ANIMALS
IN CROSS STITCH

ANIMALS
IN CROSS STITCH

Jayne Netley Mayhew
and Nicki Wheeler

David & Charles

To Ian, for every stitch that you felt,
Tim, for every word that you heard.
Thanks for all your love and support.

And a special thank you to John, for helping Jayne cross her stitches.

In loving memory of Josette,
a kind and lovely lady.

A DAVID & CHARLES BOOK

© Designs, charts and illustrations Jayne Netley-Mayhew 1995, 1998
© Text Nicki Wheeler and Jayne Netley-Mayhew 1995, 1998
© Photography David & Charles 1995, 1998

First published 1995
Reprinted 1995 (twice)
Reprinted 1996 (twice)
First published in paperback 1998

A catalogue record for this book is available from the British Library.

ISBN 0 7153 0823 8

Typeset by ABM Typographics Ltd Hull
and printed in Great Britain by Butler & Tanner Ltd
for David & Charles
Brunel House   Newton Abbot   Devon

Contents

Introduction

WE are both lucky enough to live in one of the most picturesque parts of Britain, and the rugged coastline, beautiful moorland and abundant wildlife of Devon are a joy and inspiration to us both. Consequently, we spent many hours trying to decide which animals should be included in this book, and finally settled on a rich and varied mixture to suit all tastes: a combination of countryside animals, together with some of the more exotic wildlife and birds of the world, all of which have proved to be fascinating subjects. The animals and birds included range from Siamese cats and cuddly kittens to tigers and cheetahs, from ducks and doves to exotic scarlet macaws and delicate humming-birds. Several endangered species of the world, such as elephants, pandas and whales, have also been included, and if you look hard enough you will even find insects, frogs, snails and snakes!

The book contains a range of designs and projects which are suitable for all levels of stitcher, from smaller, simpler designs for the novice to more complex projects for the 'expert'. Some of the larger designs, for example, like the spectacular pheasant with his brightly coloured plumage, or the cheetah and her cubs resting in the midday sun, are so detailed that they could easily be mistaken for paintings. This effect is achieved through a clever use of colour and stitch detail, and makes these projects an enjoyable challenge for the more experienced needleworker.

Colourful butterflies fluttering amongst hedgerow flowers and bumble bees buzzing around summer fruits can be found here decorating delightful gifts and accessories, like a scented pot-pourri pillow, pretty pincushion and fancy frilled apron. There is also a charming harvest mice spectacles case, stunning evening bag with an abstract peacock design using both silk and metallic threads, and a delightful garden bird collection, which uses the same design to make delicate cushions in pastel shades or a beautiful wool rug worked in bright, vivid colours. A wealth of inspirational ideas is included, while some of the designs are also available as kits and can be obtained by mail order – further details can be found in the stockists list at the back of the book. We hope that you will gain as much pleasure and enjoyment from working the projects in this book as we have from designing them. Happy stitching!

Techniques and Materials

FIRST STEPS: CHARTS, COLOUR KEYS AND GRAPHS

Each of the projects in this book includes a colour photograph of worked designs, colour keys, charts, graphs and instructions for making up the designs as gifts and accessories. Some designs, such as the harvest mice on page 22, have been worked on fabrics with different thread counts, making the finished stitching either larger or smaller and demonstrating just how adaptable designs and fabrics can be. You can also experiment with designs by using beads and interesting threads or simply by changing the background colour, as we have done with the humming-birds on pages 44-5.

All the designs use DMC embroidery fabrics, stranded cotton (floss) or tapestry yarn, and Twilleys metallic thread: the numbers shown on the colour key correspond to DMC shade codes. Each project lists the number of skeins required for each colour code together with a colour name, which is given for easy reference only – when purchasing threads, use the correct shade code numbers. All measurements are given in metric with the imperial equivalent in brackets. Always use either metric or imperial – do not try to mix the two.

HOW TO USE THE CHARTS

● Each chart has been hand drawn in full colour, using colours that match the thread shades as closely as possible.

● Each small coloured square on the chart represents one complete cross stitch. A half-square represents a three-quarter cross stitch. A circle or coloured dot marks the position for beads, and the thin, broken black line indicates backstitch. A French knot is represented by a small black spot (see photograph below). Small black arrows at the sides of a chart indicate the centre, and by lining these up you will be able to find the centre point.

7

• Each colour area is numbered and outlined with a thin black line (see page 7). The numbers correspond t6 those listed in the colour key at the side of each chart (see page 7).

• Some of the larger charts are spread over four pages and in these cases the colour key has been repeated on each double page.

• A 'project card' will enable you to make notes and mark stitching positions without damaging your book. Take a colour photocopy of the chart and colour key and mount them on to card. Use double-sided sticky tape to attach a length of each thread shade next to the appropriate code number on the colour key for easy reference (see photograph page 7).

• To prevent mistakes occurring, work systematically so that you read the chart accurately. Constantly check your progress against the chart and count the stitches as you go.

HOW TO USE THE COLOUR KEYS

• Each colour key has a row of coloured boxes with a number inside each box. These correspond with the colours and numbers on the relevant chart. The number at the side of each box corresponds to the DMC shade code (see photograph page 7).

HOW TO USE THE GRAPHS

• Graphs are used to indicate the placement of the designs on the fabric, as for example in the Butterfly Shawl on pages 66-9.

• Graphs have also been used to supply templates (Fig 1) for making gifts and accessories. Each square on the graph represents 5cm (2in). Transfer the template on to ready-printed dressmaker's paper, or draw up your own graph paper. All templates include a 1.5cm (⅝in) seam allowance.

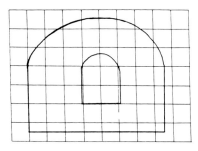

Fig 1 Template drawn up on a graph

TECHNIQUES

Cross stitch embroidery is a simple and straightforward technique: some of the designs in this book may look complicated, but the effects are achieved by the clever use of colour and stitch work. Detail is added by the use of three-quarter cross stitch, backstitch and French knots, in some cases with the addition of beads and metallic threads. The stitch diagrams in the Stitch Guide (pages 10-11) show you exactly how to work all the stitches used. The following techniques and tips will help you to achieve a professional finish by learning how to prepare your equipment and materials and then, once the cross stitching is complete, how to care for your finished work.

PREPARATION

• Cut the fabric at least 8-10cm (3-4in) larger than the finished size of the design, which is given for each project – this will allow for turnings or seam allowances when mounting the work or making it up into gifts. If making up a garment such as a waistcoat, mark out the pattern pieces on to fabric before you start stitching to ensure the correct placement of each design.

• To prevent the fabric from fraying, machine stitch around the edges or bind with tape.

• Tack (baste) a row of stitches horizontally and vertically from the centre of each side of the fabric, to find the centre point from which to start stitching.

FRAMES

• Mount the fabric on to an embroidery hoop or frame which will accommodate the whole design. Your work will be easier to handle and stitches will be kept flat and smooth.

• Bind the outer ring of an embroidery hoop with white bias tape to prevent it from marking the fabric. This will also help keep the fabric taut and prevent it from slipping.

EQUIPMENT

• Stitch up your design using a tapestry needle, which has a large eye and blunted end to prevent damage to the fabric. Choose a size of needle which will slide easily through the holes of the fabric without distorting or enlarging them. Use a thimble to avoid hurting your fingers whilst pushing the needle through the fabric. You will also need a sharp pair of embroidery scissors for snipping threads.

STARTING OFF

• To start off your first length of thread, make a knot at one end and then push the needle through to the back of the fabric, about 3cm (1¼in) from your starting point, leaving the knot on the right side. Stitch towards the knot, securing the thread at the back of the fabric as you go (Fig 2). When the thread is secure, cut off the knot. To finish off or start new threads, weave the thread into the back of worked stitches (Fig 3).

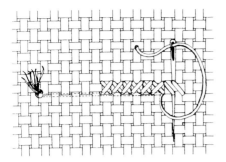

Fig 2 Starting off a thread

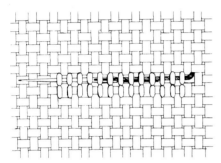

Fig 3 Weaving a thread through back of stitches

FABRICS AND THREADS

FABRICS

Most designs in this book have been worked on Aida fabric with 14 blocks or threads to 2.5cm (1in). Some designs use a larger or smaller count Aida or an even-weave fabric such as linen. One of the reasons why cross stitch is so popular, apart from its being easy to work, is that the designs are simple to adapt: merely by changing the fabric, the thickness or type of thread or the background colour a design can be transformed, and examples of this are given throughout the book. All DMC threads and fabrics can be purchased from good needlework shops.

• Some of the designs are worked on very fine fabrics such as the frog buttons (page 119) and Peacock Pendant (page 100). These can be hard work on the eyes, so to prevent eye strain you could work the design on a slightly coarser fabric, or alternatively use an illuminated magnifying glass.

• Each project lists the type of fabric used, giving the thread count, fabric name and DMC code number, which should be quoted when purchasing goods. The finished size of the designs is also given, but you can experiment by using different fabric counts to achieve surprising effects. Before starting a piece of work, always check the thread and stitch count to ensure that the design will fit the frame for which it is intended.

WASHING AND PRESSING FINISHED WORK

• If your work has become grubby during stitching, gently hand wash in warm water using a soft liquid detergent. Use a soft nail brush to remove any stubborn marks, rinse in clean water, place on a clean white towel, and leave to dry on a flat surface.

• **Do not press directly on to your work** as this will flatten the stitches and spoil the finished effect. Lay the work face down on a clean white towel, cover with a clean, fine cloth and then press.

MOUNTING AND FRAMING

• Take your finished work to a professional framer, who will be able to stretch the fabric correctly and cut any surrounding mounts accurately.

• For smaller pieces, back with lightweight iron-on interfacing to prevent the fabric wrinkling, and then mount into plastic flexi-hoops, trinket boxes or cards, following the manufacturer's instructions.

MAKING UP GARMENTS AND ACCESSORIES

• When making up any item, a 1.5cm (⅝in) seam allowance has been used unless otherwise stated.

• Instructions for making up are included under each project, where appropriate.

THREADS

If you want your designs to look exactly the same as those shown in the photographs, you must use the colours and threads listed for each project. The threads used in this book are DMC stranded cotton (floss) and tapestry wool (yarn), and Twilleys metallic thread.

• Stranded cotton (floss) is a lustrous, 'mercerised' thread, which has a smooth finish and a slight sheen. It is made from six strands twisted together to form a thick thread, which can be used whole or split into thinner strands. The type of fabric used will determine how many strands of thread you will need to use; most of the designs in this book use two strands of thread for cross stitch and one strand for backstitch. Stranded cotton (floss) is the most widely used embroidery thread and is available in nearly 400 colour shades.

• Tapestry yarn is a matt, hairy yarn made from 100 per cent wool. Short fibres are twisted together to make a single thread which cannot be split, and designs are usually worked on canvas using one or two strands. There is a wide selection of colours available, with the shades tending to be slightly duller than for stranded cotton (floss).

• Metallic threads vary quite considerably in texture and fibre content. Twilleys Goldfingering and Goldust are thick, single threads made from a mixture of viscose, nylon and metallised polyester. Finer threads are often made from metallised polyester or Lurex and have a flat appearance.

THREAD MANAGEMENT
• Always keep threads tidy and manageable. Thread organisers complete with project cards are ideal for this purpose (see page 7). Cut the threads into equal lengths and loop them into project cards, with the thread shade code written at the side. This will prevent the threads from becoming tangled and the shade codes being lost.

STITCH GUIDE

When following these instructions, please note that one block or thread refers to one block of Aida fabric or one thread of evenweave fabric.

CROSS STITCH
• Each coloured square on the chart represents one complete cross stitch.
• Cross stitch is worked in two easy stages. Start by working one diagonal stitch over one block or thread, then work a second diagonal stitch over the first stitch, but in the opposite direction, to form a cross (Fig 4).

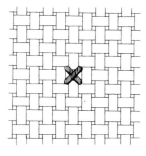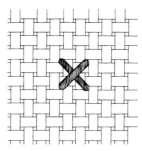

Fig 4 Completed cross stitch   *Fig 5 Cross stitch over two blocks or threads*

• The child's cot cover and cushion on pages 114 and 117 have been worked over two blocks or threads to give a larger stitch (Fig 5).

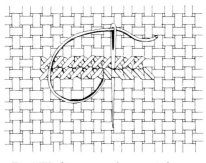

Fig 6 Working rows of cross stitches

• If you have a large area to cover, work a row of half stitches in one direction and then work back in the opposite direction with diagonal stitches to complete each cross. The upper stitches of all the crosses must lie in the same direction (Fig 6).

THREE-QUARTER CROSS STITCH
• A right-angled triangle taking up half a square on the chart represents a three-quarter cross stitch. Work the first half of the stitch in the normal way, then work the second diagonal stitch from the opposite corner but insert the needle at the centre of the cross, forming three-quarters of the complete stitch. A square showing two coloured triangles indicates that two of these stitches will have to be made back to back (Fig 7).

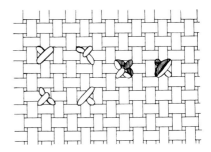

Fig 7 Three-quarter cross stitch

HALF CROSS STITCH
This stitch is only used for the peacock evening bag on pages 100-5, where detailed instructions are given on the areas to be worked. A half cross stitch is, simply, one half of a cross stitch, with the diagonal facing the same way as the upper stitches of each complete cross stitch (Fig 8).

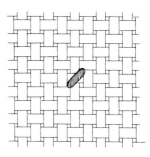

Fig 8 Half cross stitch

BACKSTITCH
Backstitch is indicated on the chart by a thin, broken black line. It is worked around areas of completed cross stitches to add definition, or on top of stitches to add

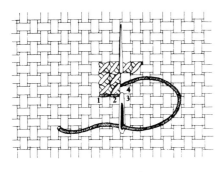

Fig 9 Backstitch

detail. To work this stitch, start by pulling the needle through the hole in the fabric at 2, then push back through at 1. For the next stitch, pull the needle through at 3, push to the back at 2, then pull the needle through to the front again at 4, ready to make the next stitch (Fig 9). This will give you short stitches at the front of your work and longer stitches at the back. If working backstitch on Afghan (Anne) even-weave fabric, work each stitch over two threads (as for cross stitch in Fig 5).

FRENCH KNOTS

These are small knots which are used to add detail, for example, the dolphin's eye on page 111. They are indicated on the charts by a small black spot. To work this stitch, bring the needle through to the front of the fabric and wind the thread tightly once around the needle. Hold the twisted thread firmly in place and carefully insert the needle one thread away from its starting position (Fig 10). For a larger knot, twist the thread two or three times around the needle.

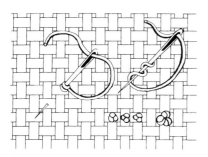

Fig 10 French knots

ADDING BEADS

Beads are indicated on the charts by a circle or coloured dot. With the needle at the right side of the fabric, thread the bead over the needle and on to the thread, then attach it to the fabric by working the first

half of the cross stitch (Fig 11). All stitches must run in the same direction so that the beads lie in neat rows on the fabric. To work up part or all of a design using beads, let each coloured square represent a bead instead of a stitch. Treat half squares as one colour and omit the backstitch detail (see the beaded spectacles case on pages 111-13).

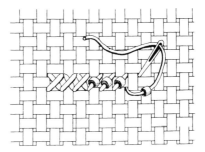

Fig 11 Adding beads

TECHNIQUE TIPS

- *Steam press the fabric before stitching to remove any stubborn creases.*
- *Always work on a frame to prevent the work becoming distorted.*
- *Work cross stitches with the top threads all facing in the same direction.*
- *Thread up lengths of several colours of stranded cotton (floss) into needles, and then arrange these at the side of your work by shade code number or colour key reference.*
- *Work the designs from the centre outwards, or split them into workable sections such as quarters. On larger designs, first work the animal and then complete the background.*
- *When taking threads across the back of a design, weave the thread through the back of existing stitches to avoid any ugly lines showing through to the right side.*
- *Use short lengths of thread (about 30cm [12in]) to minimise any knotting and tangling.*
- *Check your work constantly against the chart to avoid making mistakes.*
- *To produce a flat, smooth piece of work without any lumps or bumps, avoid using knots at the back of your work, and cut off any excess threads as short as possible.*
- *Keep your work clean by packing it away in its own clean plastic bag to prevent any nasty accidents with spilt drinks, muddy paw prints or inquisitive fingers.*

Siamese Cat Cushion and Kittens Picture

THE *elegance and sophistication of the Siamese cat is shown in these two simple designs. Both designs are worked in solid blocks of creams and browns, with bright blue for the eyes and red for the yarn. The kittens are worked using cross stitch and three-quarter cross stitch, while the adult cat includes a small amount of backstitch.*

SIAMESE CAT CUSHION

Finished design size: 28cm (11in) square approximately using Aida, 14 blocks to 2.5cm (1in)

43cm (17in) square cream Aida (Zweigart E3706), 14 blocks to 2.5cm (1in)
45cm (18in) x 115cm (45in) wide contrast cotton fabric for backing and piping
60cm (¾yd) x 115cm (45in) wide cream cotton fabric for frill
1.5m (1⅝yd) medium piping cord
25cm (10in) zip
Matching sewing thread
Paper for template
Square pad to fit cushion   (contd)

DMC STRANDED COTTON (FLOSS)

1 skein:	black 310	light coffee 422
	beige 951	red 606
	medium blue 825	light blue 800
2 skeins:	white	dark brown 898
	medium coffee 420	

1 Before you start stitching the design, read through Techniques on pages 8-9 to find out how to prepare your fabric, mark the centre point and start off your thread.

2 Match the tacking (basting) lines on the fabric with the arrows at the sides of the chart, and then work the design from the centre outwards.

3 The cross stitch and backstitch in this design are both worked using two strands of stranded cotton (floss). Refer to the Stitch Guide on pages 10-11 for instructions on working the stitches. Work backstitch detail using black 310 around the nose and mouth, beige 951 around the white outer edges of the face and red 606 for the yarn.

Fig 1 Attaching piping

Fig 2 Attaching the frill

TO MAKE UP THE CUSHION

1 For the cushion front, make a paper template measuring 40cm (16in) square. This includes a 1.5cm (⅝in) seam allowance all the way round. Pin the template on to the fabric, making sure that the embroidered design is positioned centrally, and then cut out.

2 For the cushion back, cut two pieces of contrast cotton fabric 21.5 x 40cm (8½ x 16in). With right sides facing, pin and tack (baste) the pieces together along one long edge, then stitch 7cm (2¾in) in from both ends leaving a gap at the centre. Neaten both long edges, then press seam open and insert the zip following the instructions below.

3 Using the contrast fabric, follow the instructions on page 15 to make enough covered piping to fit round the outer edge of the cushion. With the embroidered fabric facing upwards, place the covered piping around the outer edge of the cushion front, so that raw edges face outwards and stitching lines match. Pin the piping into place, allowing a little ease around each corner and overlapping the raw ends to conceal the join. Stitch into place using the zipper foot on your sewing machine. Clip the seam allowances at the corners so that they will lie flat (Fig 1).

4 For the frill, cut enough 13cm (5in) wide strips along the length of the cream fabric to give a finished length of 4.3m (4¾yd). Make the frill by following the instructions on page 15. Place the gathered frill over the piping so that all the raw edges meet. Match the pins on the frill to the corners of the fabric square and distribute the gathers evenly (Fig 2). Stitch in place carefully by hand or by using the zipper foot on your sewing machine.

5 Open the zip slightly, then lay the front and back squares together with right sides facing. Pin and tack (baste), then carefully stitch along the stitching line through all layers of fabric, using the zipper foot on your machine. Trim away excess fabric and neaten raw edges. Turn the cushion cover right side out through the zipper opening and insert the cushion pad.

TO INSERT THE ZIP

1 Complete step 2 above.

2 Place the zip on a flat surface, with right side facing. Lay the fabric, right side facing, over the zip so that the pressed seam runs along the centre of the zip. Tack (baste) along each side and both ends of the zip, and then stitch into place using the zipper foot on your sewing machine. Remove all tacking (basting) stitches (Fig 3).

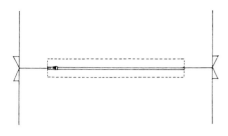

Fig 3 Inserting the zip

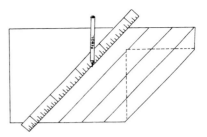

Fig 5 Marking out bias strips

TO MAKE THE FRILL

1 The fabric for a frill should measure three times the length of frill actually required (measure the outer edge of the cushion and multiply that length by three). Use a lightweight fabric which can be doubled by folding along the length to give a neat edge to the frill. To work out how wide to cut the fabric, take the finished frill width, double it, and then add the seam allowance. For the 5cm (2in) deep frill used here, double the width to give 10cm (4in), then add the seam allowance to arrive at a total width of 13cm (5in).

2 With right sides facing, stitch the fabric strips together along the short edges to form a circle. Press seams open. Fold the strip in half so that the long edges meet, enclosing the raw edges of the short seams (Fig 4). Press.

along the diagonal fold to give a bias edge. Use a pencil and ruler to mark out diagonal lines on the fabric 5cm (2in) apart, then cut along the pencil lines to make the bias strips (Fig 5).

2 With right sides facing, place the bias strips at right angles so that the short diagonal edges meet. Stitch along these edges, then press seam open (Fig 6). This process should be repeated until your strip reaches the required length.

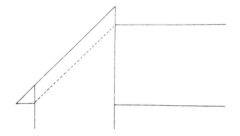

Fig 6 Joining bias strips

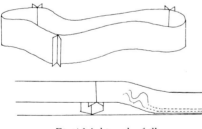

Fig 4 Making the frill

3 Run two rows of gathering threads along the raw edges of the fabric. Fold the strip into quarters by folding in half and then in half again, then mark each fold with a pin. Pull up the gathering threads until the frill is the right length, then distribute the gathers evenly.

TO MAKE THE COVERED PIPING

1 This is piping cord which has been covered with bias strips of fabric. To make the bias strips, fold over a corner of fabric at a 45° angle, then cut

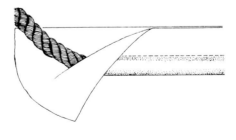

Fig 7 Covering piping cord

3 Lay the bias strip wrong side up, then place piping cord along its length. Fold the fabric in half around the cord. Use the zipper foot on your sewing machine to stitch as close to the cord as possible, so that it becomes enclosed in the fabric (Fig 7). The covered piping is now ready for use.

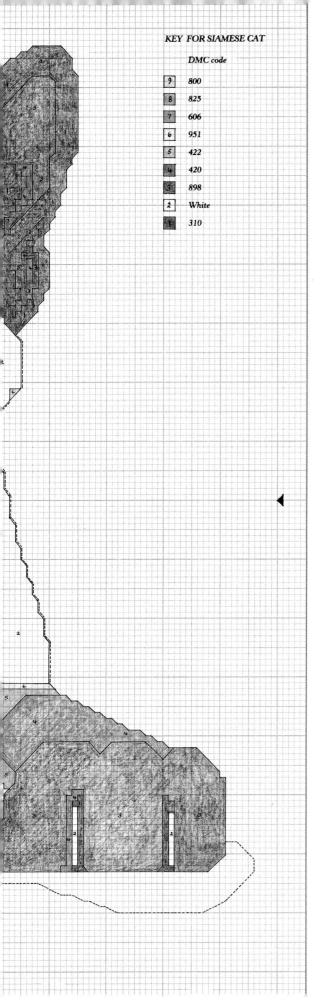

KEY FOR SIAMESE CAT

DMC code

9	800
8	825
7	606
6	951
5	422
4	420
3	898
2	White
1	310

SIAMESE KITTENS PICTURE

Finished design size: 35.5 x 40.5cm (14 x 16in) approximately using Aida, 14 blocks to 2.5cm (1in)

46 x 51cm (18 x 20in) cream Aida (Zweigart E3706), 14 blocks to 2.5cm (1in)

DMC STRANDED COTTON (FLOSS)

1 skein:	black 310	light peach 353
	rose 760	red 349
	mint green 369	medium green 320
	dark green 890	medium blue 793
	light coffee 422	medium coffee 420
	light rose 761	dark peach 351
	light green 368	medium green 367
	medium blue 794	dark blue 792
	dark brown 801	
2 skeins:	dark brown 938	beige 543
3 skeins:	white	

1 Before you start stitching the design, read through Techniques on pages 8-9 to find out how to prepare your fabric, mark the centre point and start off your thread.

2 Match the tacking (basting) lines on the fabric with the arrows at the sides of the chart, and then work the design from the centre outwards.

3 The cross stich in this design is worked using two strands of stranded cotton (floss). Refer to the Stitch Guide on pages 10-11 for instructions on working the stitches.

4 Refer to Mounting and Framing on page 9 for instructions on completing your picture.

SIAMESE CATS

*T*HE regal charm and sophistication of these cats may be due to the fact that they were originally bred and owned exclusively by the kings of Siam. In 1880, the king of Siam gave two cats to the English consul-general, who took them back to England and exhibited the pair at the Great Exhibition of 1886. It was the first time that such cats had been seen and they caused a sensation. By 1890 their popularity had spread to America, with cats being sold for prices as high as $1,000. These cats are now found worldwide, their slim physique and unique colouring making them instantly recognisable.

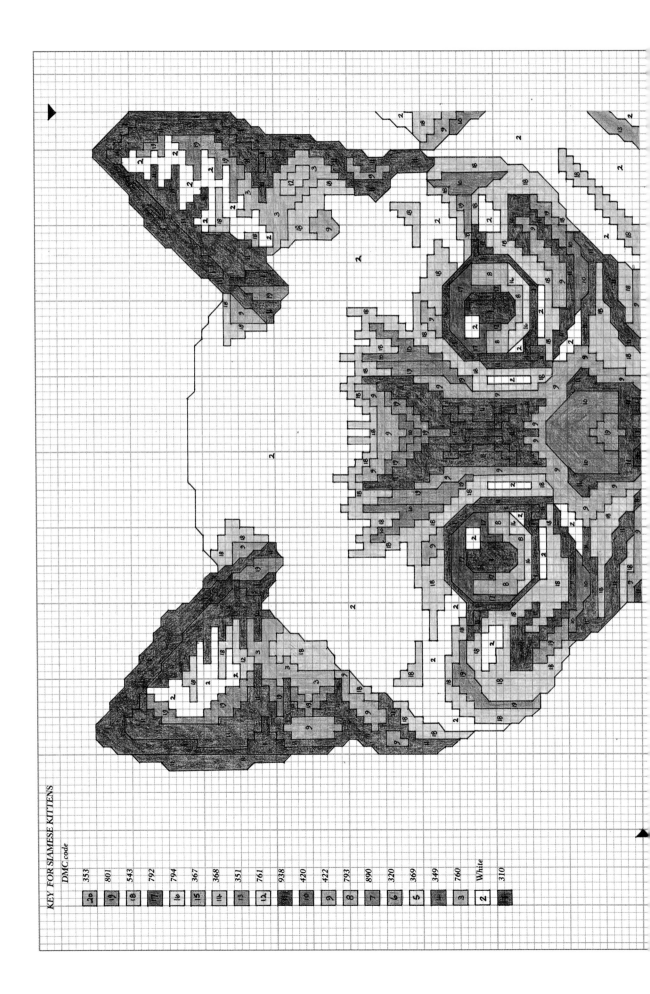

KEY FOR SIAMESE KITTENS

DMC code

	DMC
20	353
19	801
18	543
17	792
16	794
15	367
14	368
13	351
12	761
11	938
10	420
9	422
8	793
7	890
6	320
5	369
4	349
3	760
2	White
1	310

DMC code

20	353
19	801
18	543
17	792
16	794
15	367
14	368
13	351
12	761
11	938
10	420
9	422
8	793
7	890
6	320
5	369
4	349
3	760
2	White
	310

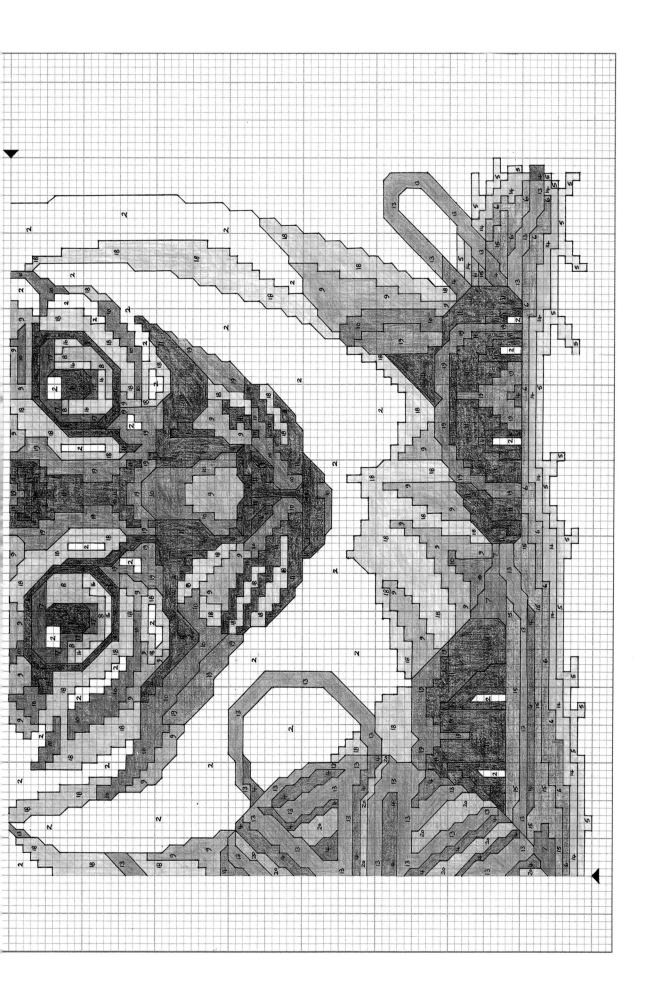

Harvest Mice Spectacles Case and Table Runner

THESE mischievous little harvest mice, scampering amongst the corn and grasses, have been captured in this colourful design. The delicate mice, bright red poppies and golden corn are beautifully framed by a border of black and gold. This project shows how versatile cross stitch can be, with the fine detail of the spectacles case being cleverly transformed into the bold image on the table runner.

HARVEST MICE SPECTACLES CASE

See chart on page 24 for finished design size, materials and threads.

1 Before you start stitching the design, read through Techniques on pages 8-9 to find out how to prepare your fabric, mark the centre point and start off your thread.
2 Match the tacking (basting) lines on the fabric with the arrows at the sides of the chart, and then work the design from the centre outwards, finishing with the border.
3 The cross stitch in this design is worked using two strands of stranded cotton (floss) and the backstitch using one strand. Refer to the Stitch Guide on pages 10-11 for instructions on working the stitches. Work backstitch detail using dark brown 898 around the eyes, ears and feet, and all around the mice and their tails.

TO MAKE UP THE SPECTACLES CASE

1 Complete the stitching of both designs and then cut away excess fabric to 1.5cm (⅝in). Cut two pieces of black felt to the same size as the front and back embroidered pieces. Press turnings to the wrong side along the top edges of the embroidered pieces.
2 With right sides facing, place front and back pieces together, matching the bottom edges. Pin, tack (baste) and then stitch along three edges, leaving the top edge open to form a pouch (Fig 1). Repeat for the felt, taking a 2cm (¾in) seam allowance. Trim all seam allowances to 6mm (¼in). Turn the embroidered pouch through to the right side.

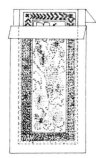

Fig 1 Stitching along three edges to form a pouch

3 Hand stitch the upholstery cord around the outer edge of the pouch, overlapping the raw ends on the top flap to conceal the join (Fig 2).

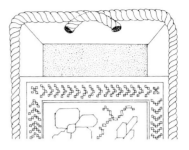

Fig 2 Attaching upholstery cord

4 With seams facing outwards, place the felt lining inside the embroidered pouch. Hand stitch the lining in place along the top edges of the pouch, and then finish by stitching a snap fastener at each corner of the flap to keep it securely in place.

HARVEST MICE TABLE RUNNER

See chart on page 25 for finished design size, materials and threads.

1 Follow steps 1 and 2 for the Spectacles Case.
2 The cross stitch in this design is worked using six strands of stranded cotton (floss) and the backstitch using two strands. Refer to the Stitch Guide on pages 10-11 for instructions on working the stitches. Work backstitch detail using dark brown 898 around the eyes, ears and feet, and all around the mice and their tails.

TO MAKE UP THE TABLE RUNNER

1 Complete the stitching of the design and then trim away excess fabric to 1.5cm (⅝in). Press carefully on the wrong side. Use matching sewing thread to machine stitch the turnings in place. Hide the machine stitching by working from the right side and stitching in the groove between the first two rows of cross stitches. Alternatively, slipstitch the turnings in place by hand.
2 Cut the felt backing to the same size as the embroidered fabric and press a small turning all the way round. Stitch furnishing fringing along both short edges of the embroidered fabric and then pin, tack (baste) and hand stitch the felt backing into place, concealing all raw edges.

HARVEST MICE SPECTACLES CASE

Finished design size:
10 x 16cm (4 x 6¼in)
approximately using
Aida, 14 blocks to
2.5cm (1in)

33 x 43 cm (13 x 17in)
 cream Aida (Zweigart
 E3706), 14 blocks to
 2.5cm (1in)
20cm (8in) square
 black felt for lining
68cm (¾yd) matching
 upholstery cord
Two small snap fasteners
Matching sewing thread

DMC STRANDED COTTON
(FLOSS)
1 skein: white
      light coffee 977
      dark tan 975
      dark peach 351
      red 321
      pale beige 677
      dark beige 680
      gold 783
      beige 945
      tan 976
      yellow 726
      red 350
      dark brown 898
      beige 729
      green 3346
2 skeins: black 310

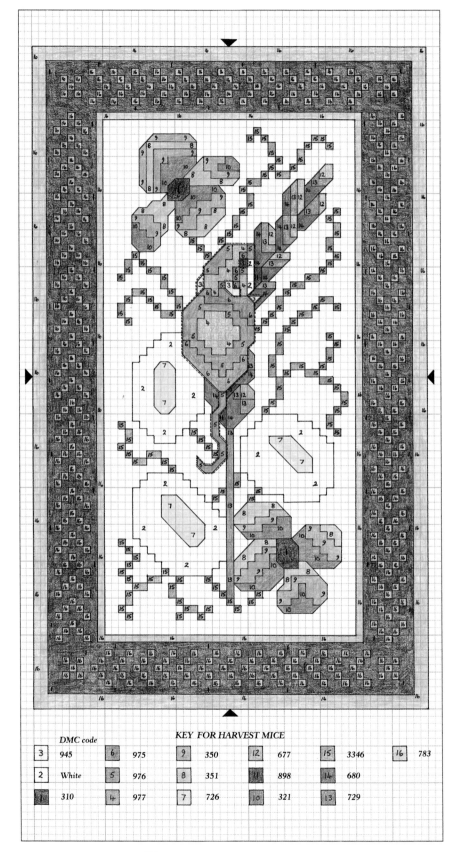

KEY FOR HARVEST MICE

	DMC code										
3	945	6	975	9	350	12	677	15	3346	16	783
2	White	5	976	8	351	11	898	14	680		
	310	4	977	7	726	10	321	13	729		

HARVEST MICE TABLE RUNNER

Finished design size:
23 x 42cm (9 x 16½in)
approximately using
fabric with 6 blocks to
2.5cm (1in)

38 x 56cm (15 x 22in)
white Zweibinca
(Zweigart E3712),
6 blocks to 2.5cm (1in)
28 x 47cm (11 x 18½in)
black felt for backing
50cm (⅝yd) gold
furnishing fringing
Matching sewing thread

DMC STRANDED COTTON
(FLOSS)
1 skein: white
           light coffee 977
           dark tan 975
           dark peach 351
           red 321
           pale beige 677
           dark beige 680
           beige 945
           tan 976
           yellow 726
           red 350
           dark brown 898
           beige 729
           green 3346
4 skeins: gold 783
5 skeins: black 310

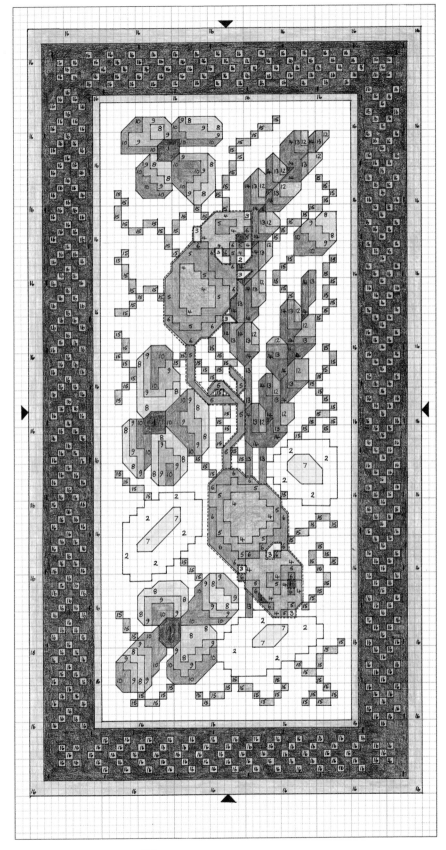

Ducks
Tea Cosy and
Table Linen

*T*HE *stylish tea cosy and tray cloth pictured here have been decorated with a brightly coloured teal wading through the reeds of a riverbank. He is just one of the duck designs in this collection of table linen. The designs are worked using a mixture of cross stitch, three-quarter cross stitch and backstitch. Detail and definition is added to the feathers by working backstitch over the top of existing stitches, while the teal design is given extra sparkle with the addition of beads to the rushes.*

TEAL TEA COSY

Finished design size: 20cm (7¾in) square approximately using Aida, 14 blocks to 2.5cm (1in)

50 x 56cm (19¾ x 22in) white Aida (Zweigart E3706), 14 blocks to 2.5cm (1in)
50 x 56cm (19¾ x 22in) cotton fabric for backing
30cm (⅜yd) x 90cm (36in) wide medium-weight polyester wadding (batting)
50cm (⅝yd) x 90cm (36in) wide lining fabric
1m (1⅛yd) matching upholstery cord
Matching sewing thread
Paper for template
One small pack tiny gold glass beads *(cont)*

DMC STRANDED COTTON (FLOSS)

1 skein:
black 310	white
dark green 986	lime green 906
pale yellow 744	orange 741
rust 720	dark buff 436
dark copper 300	dark grey 535
mid-grey 415	pale beige 677
buff 738	beige 951
dark brown 3021	light brown 3032
blue 597	airforce blue 931
mid-blue 932	pale blue 3753
sage green 522	sage green 523
light green 524	

1 Before you start stitching the design, read through Techniques on pages 8-9 to find out how to prepare your fabric, mark the centre point and start off your thread.

2 Match the tacking (basting) lines on the fabric with the arrows at the sides of the chart, and then work the design from the centre outwards. Work the teal first, then fill in the background, water and rushes.

3 The cross stitch in this design is worked using two strands of stranded cotton (floss) and the backstitch using one strand. Refer to the Stitch Guide on pages 10-11 for instructions on working the stitches and attaching beads.

4 Work backstitch detail using black 310 for the head and beak area, dark copper 300 for the shoulder, tail feathers, under-wing and rump areas, and dark buff 436 for the chest, rushes and beads. The position of each bead is indicated by a small circle on the chart. For a tray cloth, replace each bead with a cross stitch worked in dark buff 436.

TEAL

TEAL are migratory birds and may be found in fresh-water ponds and lakes, estuaries, saltmarshes and even coastal bays. The male has brightly coloured plumage with a dark chestnut head and a dark green stripe running from the eye. The female is mottled brown all over and rather dull by comparison. They breed from late spring onwards, laying their eggs in nests hidden on the ground amongst reeds and rushes. Once the female has laid her eggs, the male leaves the nest to moult.

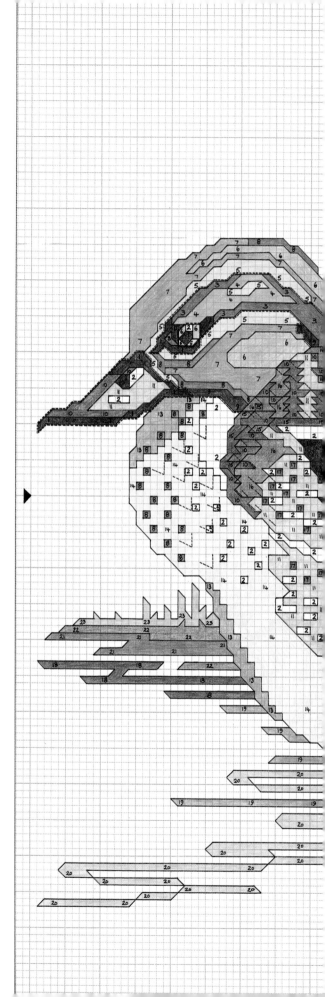

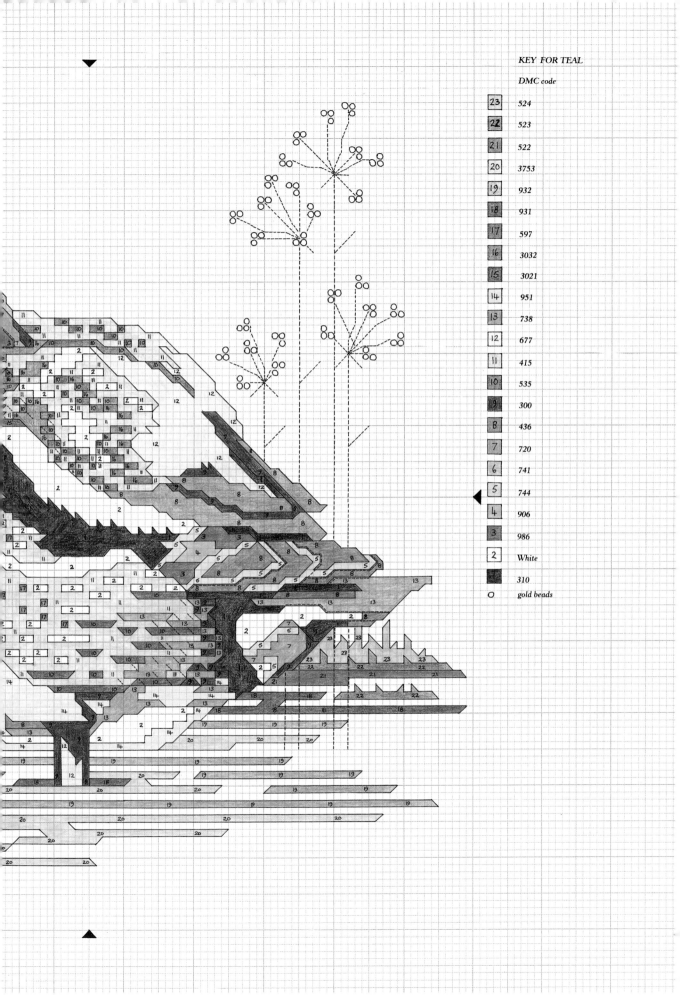

KEY FOR TEAL

DMC code

23	524
22	523
21	522
20	3753
19	932
18	931
17	597
16	3032
15	3021
14	951
13	738
12	677
11	415
10	535
9	300
8	436
7	720
6	741
5	744
4	906
3	986
2	White
■	310
O	gold beads

TO MAKE UP THE TEA COSY

1 Use the graph to draw out a template of the tea cosy pattern (Fig 1). Refer to How to Use the Graphs on page 8 for instructions. Place the template centrally over the stitched design and then cut one shape in Aida and one in cotton backing fabric. Also cut two shapes each from wadding (batting) and lining fabric.

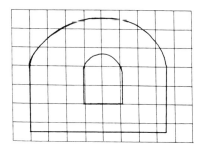

Fig 1 Template for tea cosy and egg cosy

2 Lay the wadding (batting) shapes side by side on a flat surface. With right sides up, place the embroidered Aida and the cotton backing fabric one on top of each wadding (batting) shape. Tack (baste) the fabric and wadding (batting) together to form the front and back pieces of the tea cosy.
3 With right sides facing and wadding (batting) outwards, place the front and back pieces together. Pin, tack (baste) and machine stitch round the curved edge. Trim away excess wadding (batting) to 6mm (¼in) from the seam line. Secure the wadding (batting) and fabric at the lower edge by machine stitching 1.5cm (⅝in) from the straight edges. Trim away excess wadding (batting) and then turn to the right side.
4 Pin, tack (baste) and machine stitch the lining

pieces together along the curved seam; then place the lining inside the tea cosy shape, concealing all seam edges. Pin, tack (baste) and machine stitch both layers together along the bottom straight edges, making sure to match the side seams. Neaten the bottom edge, then turn up a 2.5cm (1in) hem and slipstitch into place. To finish, slipstitch the twisted upholstery cord along the curved seam line, making a hanging loop at the centre.

MALLARD NAPKINS AND CARDS

Finished design size: 9cm (3½in) square approximately using Aida, 14 blocks to 2.5cm (1in)

For each card: 23cm (9in) square white Aida (Zweigart E3706), 14 blocks to 2.5cm (1in)
For each napkin: 36cm (14¼in) square cream Damask Aida (Zweigart E3229), 14 blocks to 2.5cm (1in)
Matching sewing thread

DMC STRANDED COTTON (FLOSS)

1 skein:		
	black 310	white
	beige 729	light grey 3024
	mid-grey 646	dark rust 919
	red 3777	dark copper 300
	grey 3023	emerald green 701
	deep emerald green 699	dark green 890
		light blue 800
	mid-blue 809	medium blue 793
	beige 676	dark beige 3045
	brown 433	dark brown 801
	dark blue 792	light tan 977
	moss green 470	moss green 937
	green 988	buff 437
	light tan 977	pale yellow 745
	pale yellow 744	dark brown 898
	yellow 726	

1 Follow steps 1 and 2 on page 28, working the design from the centre outwards.
2 The cross stitch in this design is worked using two strands of stranded cotton (floss) and the backstitch using one strand. Refer to the Stitch Guide on pages 10-11 for instructions on working the stitches. Work backstitch detail using dark brown 898 around each duck and green 988 for the grass.

Ducks Cards, Egg Cosies and Tea Towel

MALLARD

MALLARD *like to form small flocks by still- and fresh-water lakes, but can also be found in sheltered coastal bays and estuaries. The male has a brightly coloured bottle-green head, narrow white collar and a yellow bill; the female is dull mottled brown with orange legs and a dark bill with orange sides. In late autumn the birds pair up, to breed in late spring. Nest sites vary from foliage on the ground to trees and even birdboxes. After breeding the male moults and looks very similar to the female.*

TO MAKE UP THE NAPKINS

1 Neaten the edges of each damask square and then press a 1.5cm (⅝in) turning all the way round. Carefully mitre the corners (Fig 2), pin the hem in place and then stitch by hand or machine.

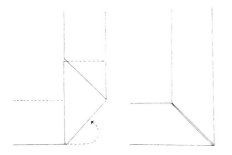

Fig 2 Mitring corners

2 Stitch a chick design in the bottom right-hand corner, 3cm (1¼in) in from the finished edges. Complete the design by adding a border consisting of a double row of cross stitches to the two outer edges. Each row is made up of 23 crosses stitched on alternate blocks. Use moss green 937 for the inner row and moss green 470 for the outer row (see photograph below).

SHELDUCK EGG COSIES AND TEA TOWEL

These four designs could be used to decorate a complete set of table linen such as napkins, a tray cloth or a tablecloth. The adults are shown on the egg cosies in the main picture on page 31, and the chicks can be found in the photographs opposite.

Finished design size: 9cm (3½in) square approx. using Aida, 14 blocks to 2.5cm (1in)

For the egg cosies: 23cm (9in) square white Aida (Zweigart E3706), 14 blocks to 2.5cm (1in)
  Matching sewing thread, scraps of lining, wadding (batting) and contrast braid
  Paper for template
For the tea towel: 49.5 x 71cm (19½ x 28in) blue Nina (Zweigart E7534) with Aida strip, 8 blocks to 2.5cm (1in)

DMC STRANDED COTTON (FLOSS)
Egg cosies
1 skein:

black 310	white
red 321	red 606
deep moss green 934	dark green 986
lime green 905	copper 301
rust 720	light rust 922
deep brown 838	dark brown 839

rose pink 758	mid-grey 451
grey 453	blue 799
mid-blue 794	light blue 800
light coffee 422	dark brown 801
mid-brown 841	buff 437
beige 676	

Tea towel

1 skein:	dark brown 838	mid-grey 451
	grey 453	light coffee 422
	dark brown 801	mid-brown 841
2 skeins:	black 310	white

EGG COSIES

1 Follow steps 1 and 2 on page 28, working the designs from the centre outwards.

2 The cross stitch in these designs is worked using two strands of stranded cotton (floss) and the backstitch using one strand. Refer to the Stitch Guide on pages 10-11 for instructions on working the stitches.

3 For each chick, work backstitch detail using dark brown 938 all around the body, wings and eye. Work the seagulls using black 310.

4 For the adults, work backstitch detail using dark brown 938 around the body and beak, and then work the eye in white.

5 Use the graph in Fig 1 for the Teal Tea Cosy to draw out a template of the egg cosy shape.

6 Follow the instructions for making up the tea cosy given on page 30. In this case, take a 6mm (¼in) seam allowance all the way round and a 1cm (½in) hem along the bottom edges.

Shelduck Chicks Stitched on Aida fabric (Opposite) Corners of Mallard Napkins

TEA TOWEL

1 This design is worked on Nina (Zweigart E7534), which has an Aida strip running through it on which to work your design. Use the chart for the shelduck chicks, working the chicks only and omitting the background.

2 Follow steps 1 and 2 for the Teal Tea Cosy, working the design from the centre outwards.

3 The cross stitch in this design is worked using three strands of stranded cotton (floss) and the backstitch using one strand. Refer to the Stitch Guide on pages 10-11 for instructions on working the stitches.

SHELDUCK

SHELDUCK *can be found in almost every coastal bay in the British Isles and Northern Europe. Both male and female have the same unmistakable bold black, white and chestnut markings. At high tide the birds rest on the sea or shore, waiting for the tide to retreat so that they can feast on mussels and crabs. Each year they migrate to northern Germany to moult their flight feathers. Only the fledglings are left behind, forming large crèches under the care of a few adults.*

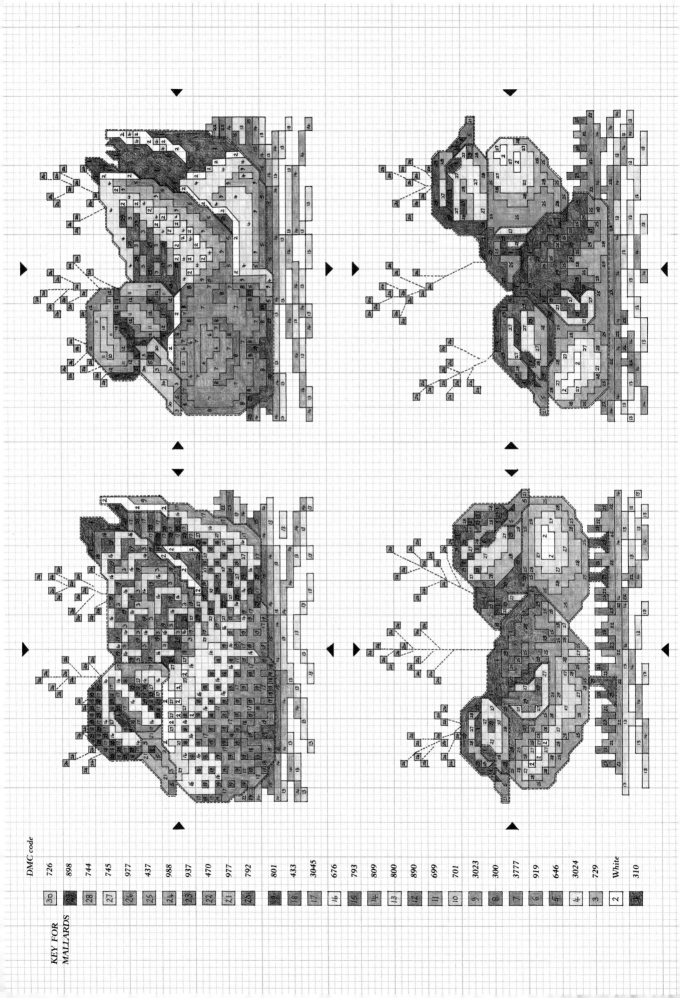

KEY FOR MALLARDS

DMC code

	DMC code
30	726
29	898
28	744
27	745
26	977
25	437
24	988
23	937
22	470
21	977
20	792
19	801
18	433
17	3045
16	676
15	793
14	809
13	800
12	890
11	699
10	701
9	3023
8	300
7	3777
6	919
5	646
4	3024
3	729
2	White
	310

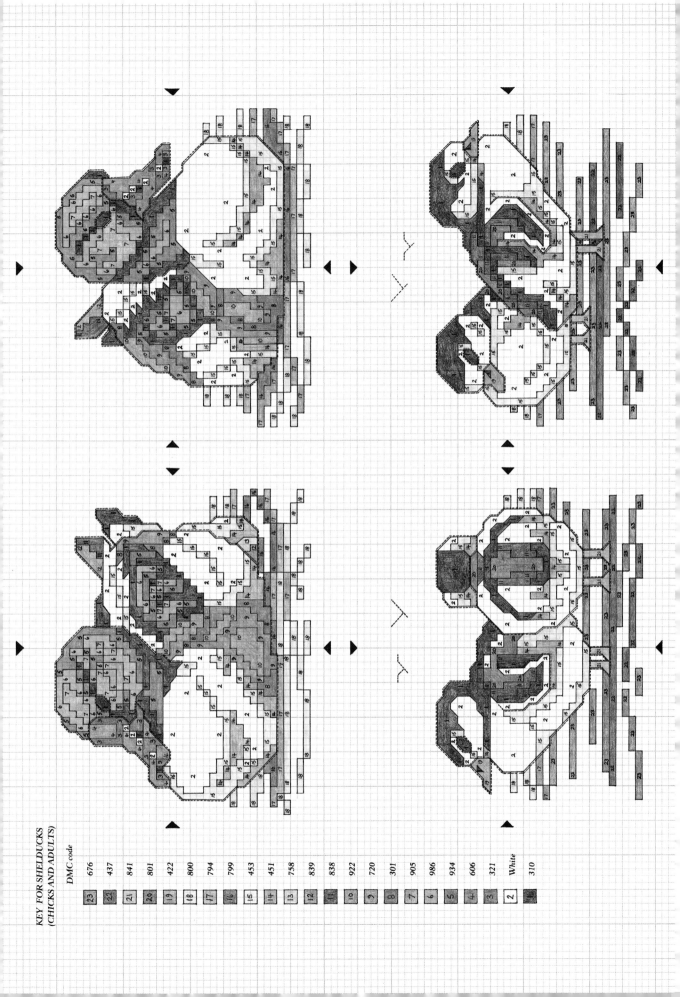

KEY FOR SHELDUCKS
(CHICKS AND ADULTS)

DMC code

23		676
22		437
21		841
20		801
19		422
18		800
17		794
16		799
15		453
14		451
13		758
12		839
11		838
10		922
9		720
8		301
7		905
6		986
5		934
4		606
3		321
2		White
1		310

Zebra Head

THIS magnificent zebra on the grassy plains of Africa makes an excellent companion to the elephant family on the following pages. The design is worked using cross stitch, three-quarter cross stitch and backstitch. The black-and-white stripes of the zebra contrast well with the lush green grass and cobalt blue sky: the striking effect is achieved by working solid blocks of colour, with only a small amount of backstitch detail, making it an ideal project for beginners.

Finished design size: 17 x 24cm (6¾in x 9½in) approximately using Aida, 14 blocks to 2.5cm (1in)

38 x 46cm (15 x 18in) white Aida (Zweigart E3706), 14 blocks to 2.5cm (1in)

DMC STRANDED COTTON (FLOSS)

1 skein:	dark brown 898	brown 433
	mid-brown 840	grey 3022
	grey 3023	light grey 3024
	light blue 800	mid-blue 809
	light green 772	mid-green 3364
	green 3363	dark green 3362
	moss green 469	dark moss green 936
	dark moss green 935	dark brown 3371
2 skeins:	black 310	white

1 Before you start stitching the design, read through Techniques on pages 8-9 to find out how to prepare your fabric, mark the centre point and start off your thread.

2 Match the tacking (basting) lines on the fabric with the arrows at the sides of the chart, and then work the design from the centre outwards. Work the zebra head first, then fill in the background area and frame surrounding the design.

3 The cross stitch in this design is worked using two strands of stranded cotton (floss), and backstitch using one strand. Refer to the Stitch Guide on pages 10-11 for instructions on working the stitches. Work backstitch detail using black 310 around the edge of the zebra head.

4 Refer to Mounting and Framing on page 9 for instructions on completing your picture.

ZEBRA

THIS temperamental black-and-white striped animal is a member of the horse family. Females and their young form small family groups which are led by an older male, who is replaced by a younger male when he becomes too old. The older male then wanders off to live on his own until he dies. Several families may live in the same area and herd together, but they all recognise each other by voice and pattern. Unfortunately, due to trophy hunting, zebra numbers have dwindled and these distinctive animals are now rare.

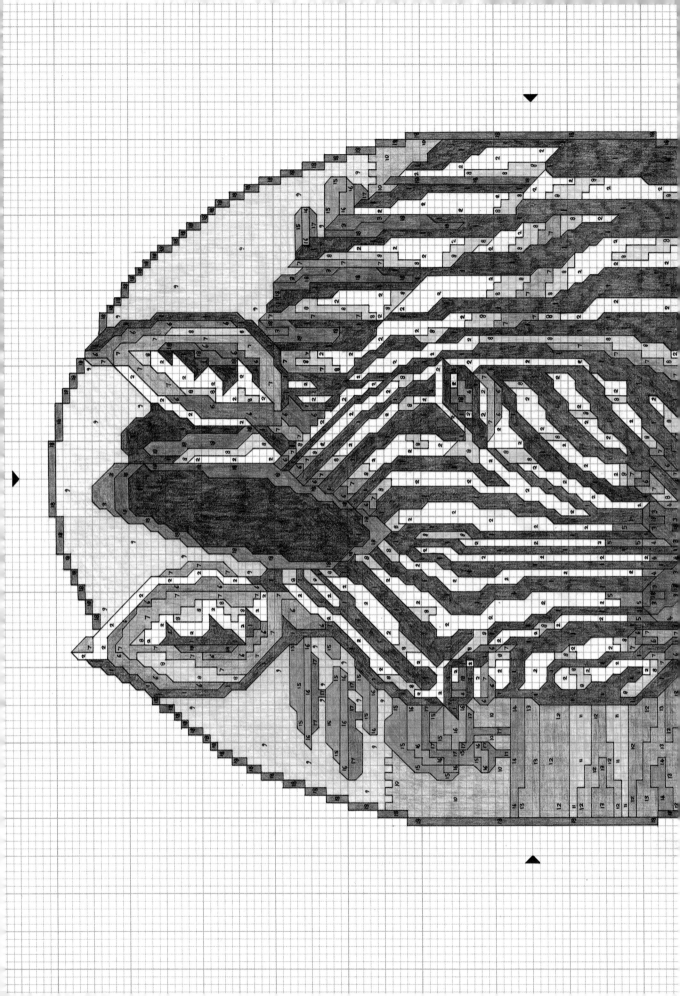

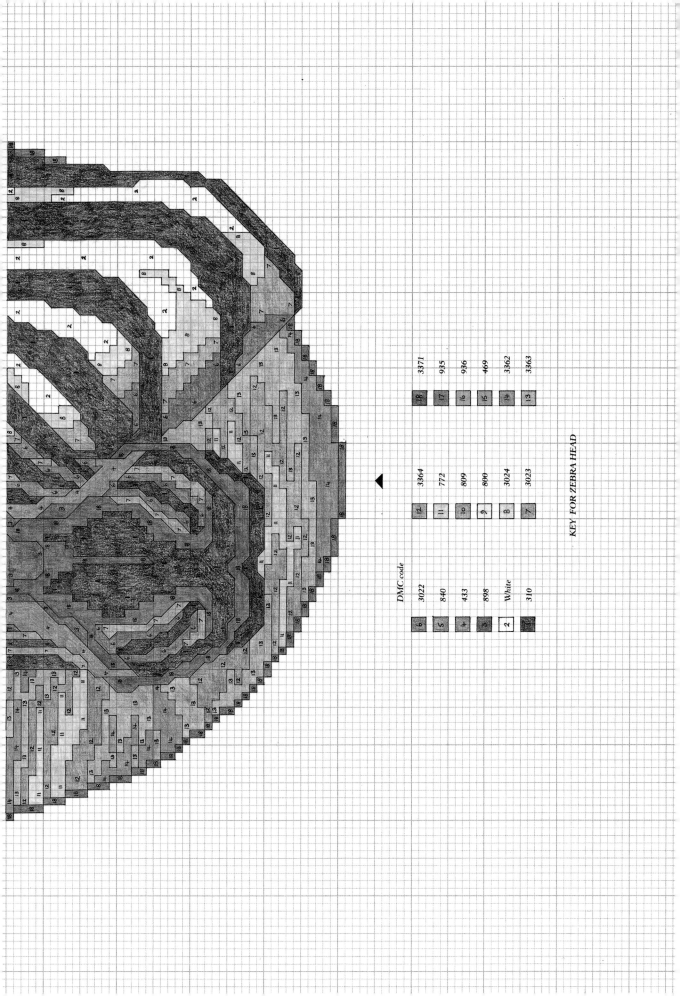

DMC code

6	3022
5	840
4	433
3	898
2	White
1	310

12	3364
11	772
10	809
9	800
8	3024
7	3023

18	3371
17	935
16	936
15	469
14	3362
13	3363

KEY FOR ZEBRA HEAD

Family of Elephants

*T*HIS *attractive picture captures beautifully the close physical bond that develops within elephant families. The large bull elephant in the foreground rears up his trunk out of the frame of the picture, whilst the females huddle in the background, protecting the young calf. The design is worked completely in cross stitch and three-quarter cross stitch, with solid blocks and lines of colour built up to create this stunning image.*

Finished design size: 16 x 25cm (6¼ x 9¾in) approximately using Aida, 14 blocks to 2.5cm (1in)

31 x 41cm (12¼ x 16¼in) white Aida (Zweigart E3706), 14 blocks to 2.5cm (1in)

DMC STRANDED COTTON (FLOSS)

1 skein:
black 310	white
dark brown 3371	deep grey 844
dark grey 645	mid-grey 646
grey 647	grey 648
mushroom 644	light blue 3325
dark green 3362	green 3363
light green 3364	khaki 371
dark mushroom 610	moss green 469
dark moss green 936	

1 Before you start stitching the design, read through Techniques on pages 8-9 to find out how to prepare your fabric, mark the centre point and start off your thread.
2 Match the tacking (basting) lines on the fabric with the arrows at the sides of the chart, and then work the design from the centre outwards. Work the large elephant, fill in the background area and then finish with the frame.
3 The cross stitch in this design is worked using two strands of stranded cotton (floss). Refer to the Stitch Guide on pages 10-11 for instructions on working the stitches.
4 Refer to Mounting and Framing on page 9 for instructions on completing your picture.

ELEPHANTS

*A*LTHOUGH *elephants are the largest living land mammals, they have a reputation for being gentle giants. They are very social animals who roam in large family troops, led by a matriarch. Each animal may consume up to 200kg (440lb) of vegetation a day. Although they can be found in forest and open grasslands, they particularly enjoy swampy areas where they can drink, play and wallow in the mud which protects their skin from parasites. Sadly, although the elephant is an endangered species, it is still ruthlessly hunted by poachers who supply the illegal ivory trade.*

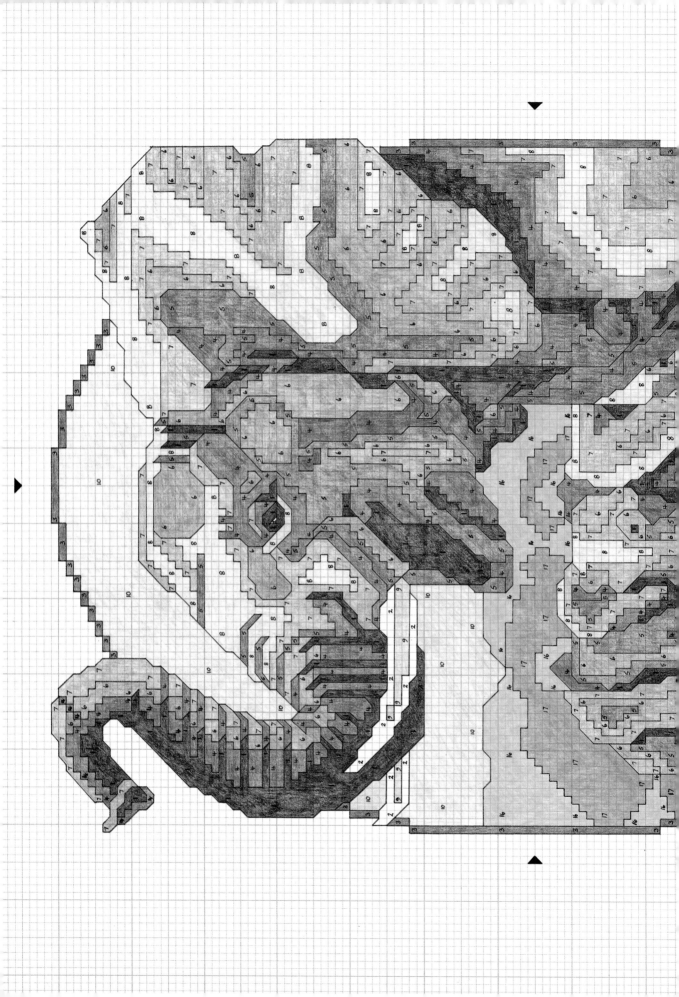

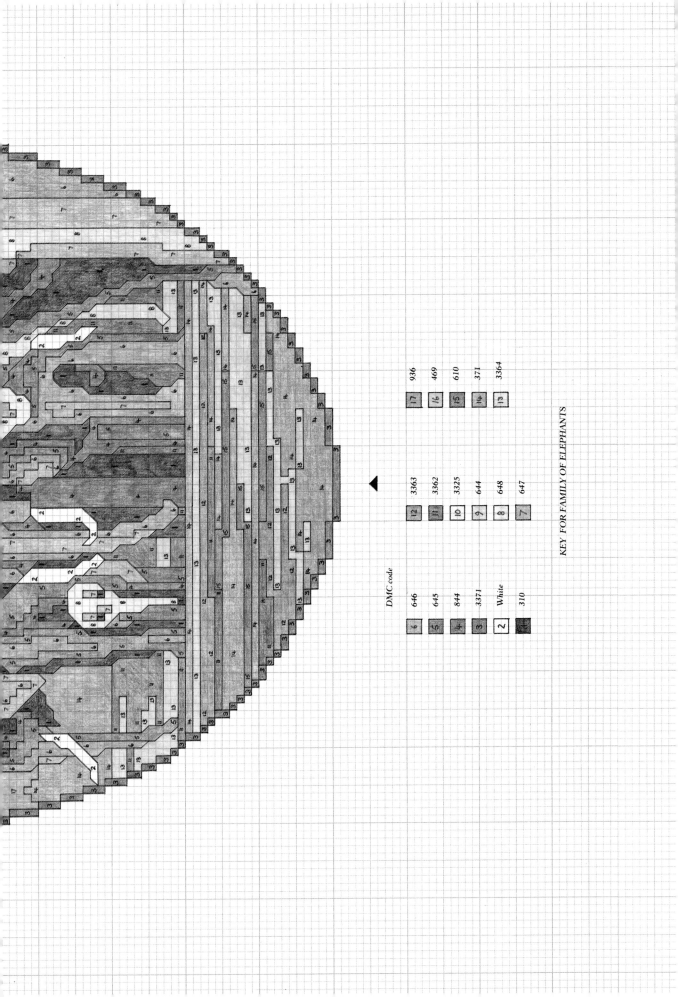

DMC code

6	646	12	3363	17	936
5	645	11	3362	16	469
4	844	10	3325	15	610
3	3371	9	644	14	371
2	White	8	648	13	3364
	310	7	647		

KEY FOR FAMILY OF ELEPHANTS

Humming-bird Cushion and Footstool

*T*HIS *spectacular design of brightly coloured humming-birds has been used to make both a cushion and footstool. The sumptuous colour and rich detail have been achieved by using over sixty shades of stranded cotton (floss). The design is worked on both cream and black Aida to show the effect that can be achieved by using a different-coloured background.*

HUMMING-BIRD CUSHION

Finished design size: 35.5cm (14in) diameter approximately using Aida, 14 blocks to 2.5cm (1in)

51cm (20in) square cream 14 count Aida (Zweigart E3706), 14 blocks to 2.5cm (1in)
45cm (18in) x 115cm (45in) wide contrast cotton fabric for backing and piping
1.8m (2yd) medium piping cord
25cm (10in) zip
Matching sewing thread
Paper for template
Circular cushion pad to fit

DMC STRANDED COTTON (FLOSS)

1 skein:
black 310	white
ecru	olive green 581
dark olive green 580	turquoise 996
dark turquoise 995	light green 3348
green 3346	sage green 522
pale beige 3047	dark beige 3045
light blue 747	light rust 922
rust 920	lime green 907
dark green 890	beige 3046
light green 772	green 3347
dark green 3345	emerald green 702
dark emerald green 700	mid-brown 841
	dark brown 839
bright pink 893	medium rose 3328
light emerald green 703	emerald green 701
	deep emerald green 699
dull green 503	
dark green 501	deep green 500
beige 543	mid-brown 840
dark salmon 3705	light mint green 955
mint green 912	dark green 910
lime green 906	sage green 523
khaki green 3051	mint green 954

2 skeins: deep moss green 934

Background

1 skein:
flesh 754	peach 352
light red 350	green 989
dark green 895	mid-grey 451
deep yellow 743	lilac 210
dark lilac 208	deep purple 550
light moss green 471	moss green 470
moss green 937	lilac 211
lilac 209	dark purple 552
dark green 987	grey 452
flesh 948	red 817

2 skeins:
grey 453	dark peach 351
red 349	

1 Before you start stitching the design, read through Techniques on pages 8-9 to find out how to prepare your fabric, mark the centre point and start off your thread.

2 Match the tacking (basting) lines on the fabric with the arrows at the sides of the chart, and then work the design from the centre outwards.

3 Both the cross stitch and backstitch in this design are worked using two strands of stranded cotton (floss). Refer to the Stitch Guide on pages 10-11 for instructions on working the stitches.

4 For the pink- and white-throated birds, work backstitch detail around the wings and tail feathers using deep moss green 934, and for the deep blue- and rust-throated birds, work backstitch detail around the wings and tail feathers using black 310. For the background, work backstitch detail around the flower stamens using dark brown 839.

If you wish to mount the design into a circular footstool, work the design without the hexagonal border.

TO MAKE UP THE CUSHION

1 For the cushion front, use a pencil to mark 2.5cm (1in) from the border all the way round the design. Cut away any excess fabric along this line. This will allow for a 1.5cm (⅝in) seam allowance and enough ease to fit a circular cushion pad.

2 For the cushion back, transfer the template (Fig 1) on to graph paper. Refer to How to Use the Graphs on page 8 for instructions. Then, cut two shapes from the contrast fabric. With right sides facing, pin and tack (baste) the long edges together, then stitch 6cm (2¼in) in from both ends, leaving a gap at the centre. Press seam open and insert the zip, following the instructions for the Siamese Cat Cushion on page 14.

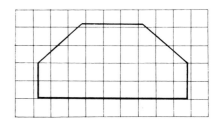

Fig 1 Template for cushion

3 Make enough ruched piping to fit around the outer edge of the cushion, following the instructions given opposite.

4 With the embroidered fabric facing upwards, place the piping, with raw edges facing outwards, around the outer edge of the cushion, making sure that stitching lines match. Pin the piping into place, allowing a generous amount of ease at each corner. Overlap the raw ends to conceal the join. Stitch in place using the zipper foot on your sewing machine, or alternatively by hand. Clip the seam allowances at the corners so that the corners will lie flat (Fig 2).

5 With the zip slightly open, lay the front and

Fig 2 Attaching ruched piping

back pieces together with right sides facing. Pin, tack (baste) and stitch along the stitching line through all layers of fabric either by hand or machine. Trim away any excess fabric and neaten raw edges. Turn the cushion cover to the right side through the zipper opening and insert the cushion pad.

TO MAKE THE RUCHED PIPING

1 This is piping cord covered with bias strips of fabric, which is then ruched along its length. To make bias strips, follow steps 1 and 2 of the instructions for the Siamese Cat Cushion given on page 15, but cut the strips 8cm (3in) wide. To allow for the ruching, the finished strip should be between two and three times longer than the actual length required.

2 Lay the bias strip wrong side up and place the piping cord along its length. Fold the fabric in half around the cord. Use a normal foot on your sewing machine and set the needle to a wide position, so that the stitching line will lie further away from the cord – this will allow enough ease for ruching the fabric over the cord. Stitch along the length of the cord to enclose it inside the fabric.

3 Stitch the piping cord securely at one end of the bias fabric and then gather the fabric along the length of the cord to form ruches (Fig 3). Ruche the fabric to the desired length and distribute the ruches evenly. Cut off excess piping cord, leaving a length of about 13cm (5in) to allow for ease around the corners. The ruched piping cord is now ready for use.

HUMMING-BIRD FOOTSTOOL

Finished design size: 33cm (13in) diameter
approximately using Aida, 14 blocks to 2.5cm (1in)

51cm (20in) square black Aida (Zweigart E3706), 14 blocks to 2.5cm (1in)
35.5cm (14in) diameter circular footstool

1 Follow the list of stranded cotton (floss) requirements and the instructions on how to stitch up the design given for the Humming-bird Cushion.
2 If you wish to mount this design in a circular footstool, it is advisable to omit the hexagonal border.
3 When working up the design on black Aida, omit greys 451, 452 and 453 for the background area. These are shades of dark grey which do not show up on the black fabric.
4 Refer to Mounting and Framing on page 9 for instructions on completing your footstool.

HUMMING-BIRDS

*T*HERE *are many species of these tiny, brightly coloured birds, including the smallest known bird in the world which measures only 6cm (2 1/4in) long. Humming-birds are found in the Americas from the Andes to Alaska, and in virtually any habitat from forest to desert. They are named after the noise produced by the rapid wing beat which allows for precision hovering in any direction. They feed by hovering next to a flower and using their long, thin bills and elongated, tubular tongues to suck up nectar.*

Fig 3 Ruching fabric over piping cord

KEY FOR HUMMING BIRDS

DMC code

19	3046	34	500	44	954
18	890	33	501	43	3051
17	907	32	503	42	523
16	920	31	699	41	906
15	922	30	701	40	910
14	747	29	703	39	912
13	3045	28	3328	38	955
12	3047	27	893	37	3705
11	934	26	839	36	840
10	522	25	841	35	543
9	3346	24	700		
8	3348	23	702		
7	995	22	3345		
6	996	21	3347		
5	580	20	772		
4	581				
3	Ecru				
2	White				
	310				

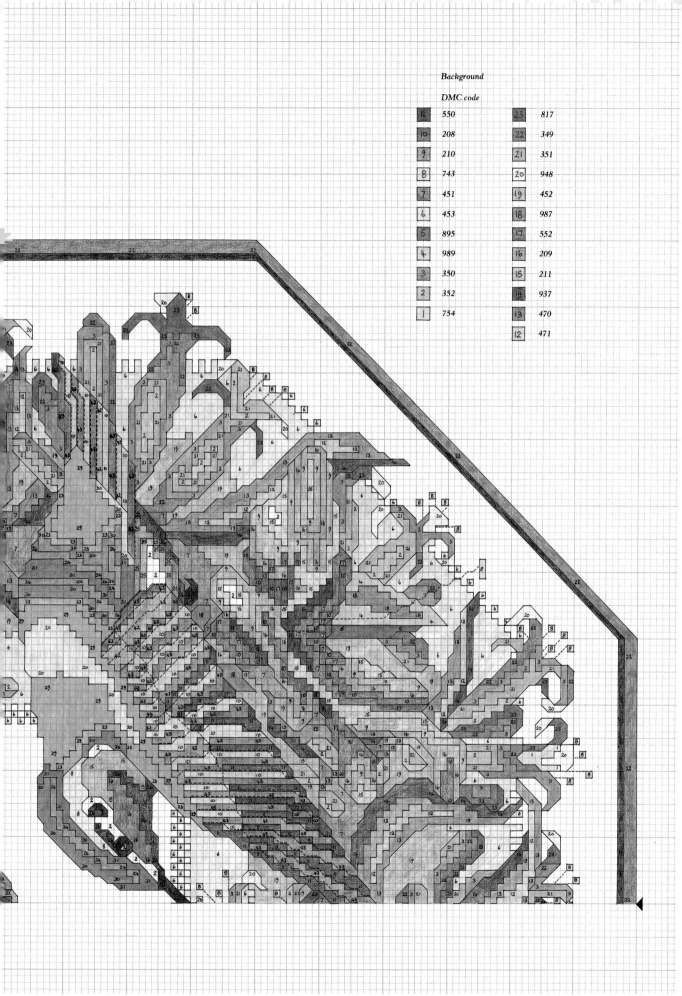

Background

DMC code

11	550		23	817
10	208		22	349
9	210		21	351
8	743		20	948
7	451		19	452
6	453		18	987
5	895		17	552
4	989		16	209
3	350		15	211
2	352		14	937
1	754		13	470
			12	471

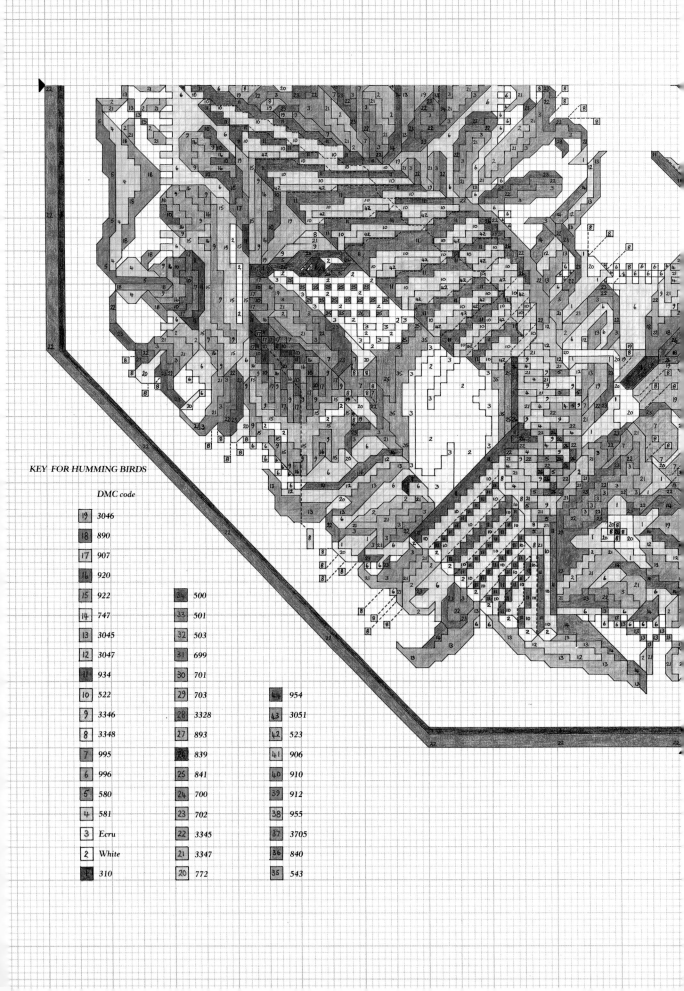

KEY FOR HUMMING BIRDS

DMC code

19	3046
18	890
17	907
16	920
15	922
14	747
13	3045
12	3047
11	934
10	522
9	3346
8	3348
7	995
6	996
5	580
4	581
3	Ecru
2	White
1	310

34	500
33	501
32	503
31	699
30	701
29	703
28	3328
27	893
26	839
25	841
24	700
23	702
22	3345
21	3347
20	772

44	954
43	3051
42	523
41	906
40	910
39	912
38	955
37	3705
36	840
35	543

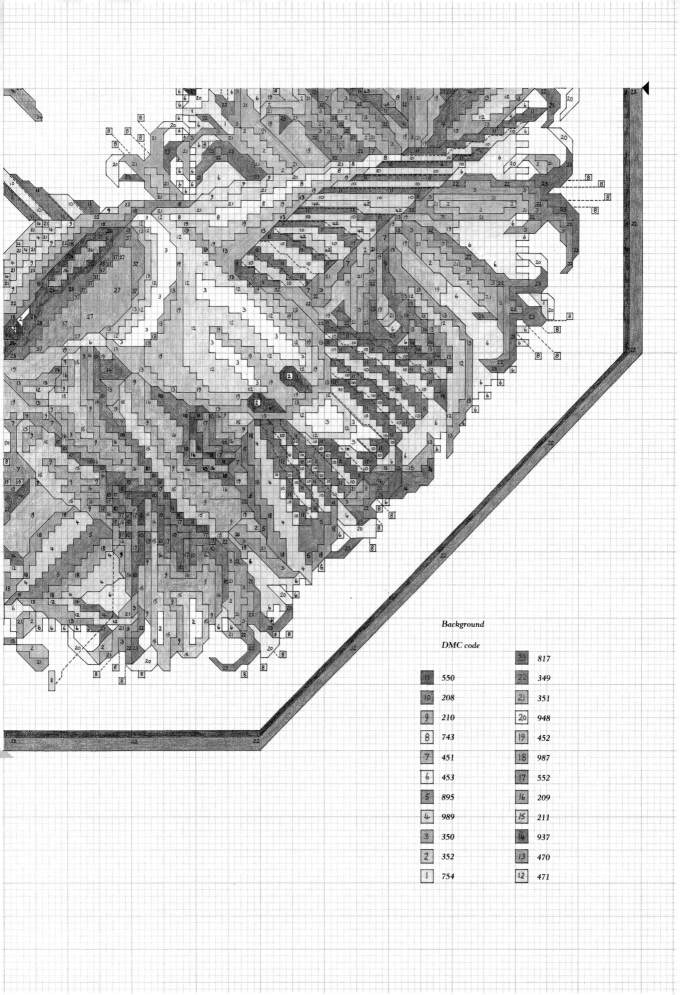

Background

DMC code

		817
11	550	23
10	208	22 349
9	210	21 351
8	743	20 948
7	451	19 452
6	453	18 987
5	895	17 552
4	989	16 209
3	350	15 211
2	352	14 937
1	754	13 470
		12 471

Scarlet Macaws

A BRIGHTLY *coloured pair of macaws is brilliantly set off against a black background fabric, which makes the colours really stand out and also saves work because you do not have to stitch the black areas on the chart. Although the design looks complicated, each colour is simply worked in solid blocks or lines using cross stitch and three-quarter cross stitch. Only the eyes are outlined in backstitch.*

Finished design size: 19 x 36cm (7½ x 14¼in) approximately using Aida, 14 blocks to 2.5cm (1in)

33 x 51cm (13 x 20in) black Aida (Zweigart E3706), 14 blocks to 2.5cm (1in)

DMC STRANDED COTTON (FLOSS)

1 skein:		
	black 310	white
	lemon 445	deep red 902
	dark red 304	red 321
	bright red 666	red 606
	deep orange 608	orange 740
	mid-grey 646	deep grey 844
	beige 951	buff 437
	dark blue 796	blue 798
	mid-blue 809	light gold 725
	yellow 726	pale lemon 3078
	olive green 581	lime green 907
	lime green 905	dark mushroom 610
	mid-brown 370	mushroom 612
	mushroom 613	

1 Before you start stitching the design, read through Techniques on pages 8-9 to find out how to prepare your fabric, mark the centre point and start off your thread.

2 Match the tacking (basting) lines on the fabric with the arrows at the sides of the chart, and then work the design from the centre outwards.

3 The cross stitch in this design is worked using three strands of stranded cotton (floss), and the backstitch using one strand. Refer to the Stitch Guide on pages 10-11 for instructions on working the stitches. Work backstitch detail using deep grey 844 around the yellow and white edges of the eyes only.

4 Refer to Mounting and Framing on page 9 for instructions on completing your picture.

SCARLET MACAWS

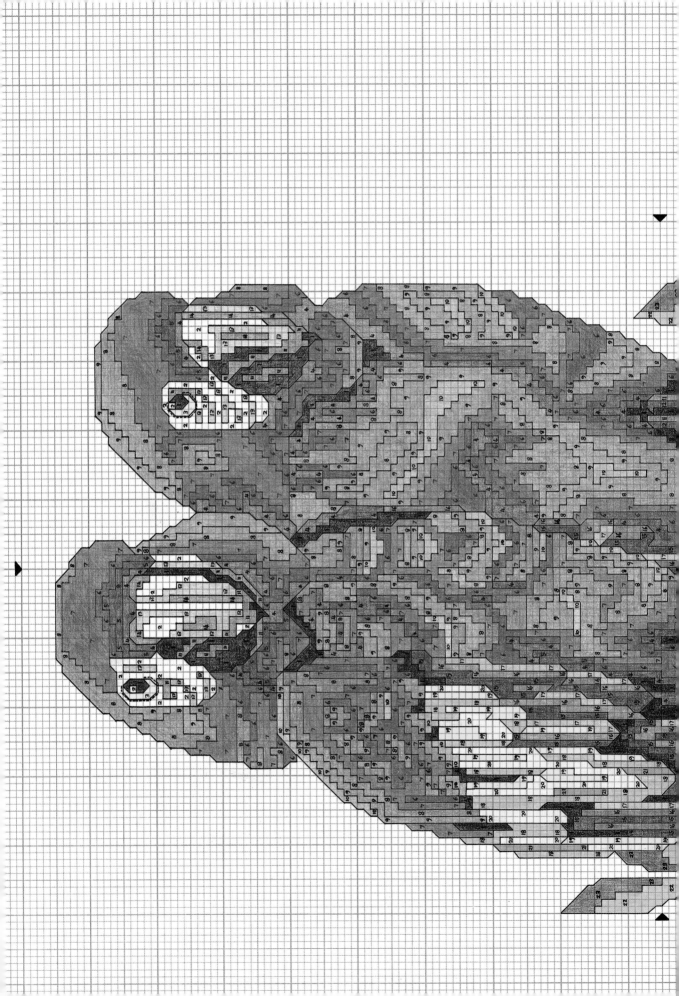

KEY FOR SCARLET MACAWS

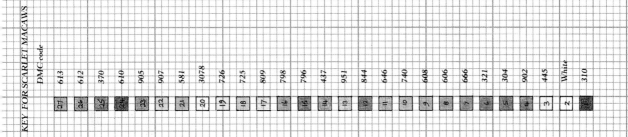

Walking Tiger

*T*HIS *picture of a tiger strolling confidently through the undergrowth captures the power and majesty of this spectacular beast, the largest of all the cat family. His distinctive deep-orange coat with dark vertical stripes makes him instantly recognisable. The design is worked completely in cross stitch and three-quarter cross stitch, with the whiskers added later in long straight stitches, making this a suitable project for stitchers of all levels.*

Finished design size: 22 x 36cm (8¾ x 14¼in) approximately using Aida, 14 blocks to 2.5cm (1in)

38 x 51cm (15 x 20in) cream Aida (Zweigart E3706), 14 blocks to 2.5cm (1in)

DMC STRANDED COTTON (FLOSS)

1 skein:	buff 437	deep buff 435
	copper 301	dark copper 300
	dark brown 938	light brown 3032
	pale brown 3033	cream 712
	rose pink 758	buff 738
2 skeins:	black 310	white

Background

1 skein:	light brown 842	mid-brown 841
	dark brown 839	mint green 369
	light green 368	medium green 367
	dark moss green 935	moss green 937
	moss green 469	moss green 470
	light moss green 471	pale moss green 472

1 Before you start stitching the design, read through Techniques on pages 8-9 to find out how to prepare your fabric, mark the centre point and start off your thread.

2 Match the tacking (basting) lines on the fabric with the arrows at the sides of the chart, and then work the design from the centre outwards. Work the tiger, then fill in the background.

3 The cross stitch in this design is worked using two strands of stranded cotton (floss). Refer to the Stitch Guide on pages 10-11 for instructions on working the stitches. The whiskers are worked with long straight stitches using one strand of white stranded cotton (floss).

4 Refer to Mounting and Framing on page 9 for instructions on completing your picture.

TIGERS

*T*IGERS *are solitary animals which can live for up to twenty-six years in their natural environment. They feed on buffalo and other large prey, and have been known to kill elephant and rhinoceros calves, but if nothing else is available they will eat frogs and locusts. The male takes no part in the upbringing of the young, which are born blind and fully furred. Unfortunately, due to the deforestation of their natural habitat, the fur trade and for use as an aphrodisiac in some oriental medicines, the tiger has become an endangered species.*

KEY FOR WALKING TIGER

Tiger

DMC code

12		738
11		758
10		712
9		3033
8		3032
7		938
6		300
5		301
4		435
3		437
2	White	
1		310

Background

DMC code

12		472
11		471
10		470
9		469
8		937
7		935
6		367
5		368
4		369
3		839
2		841
1		842

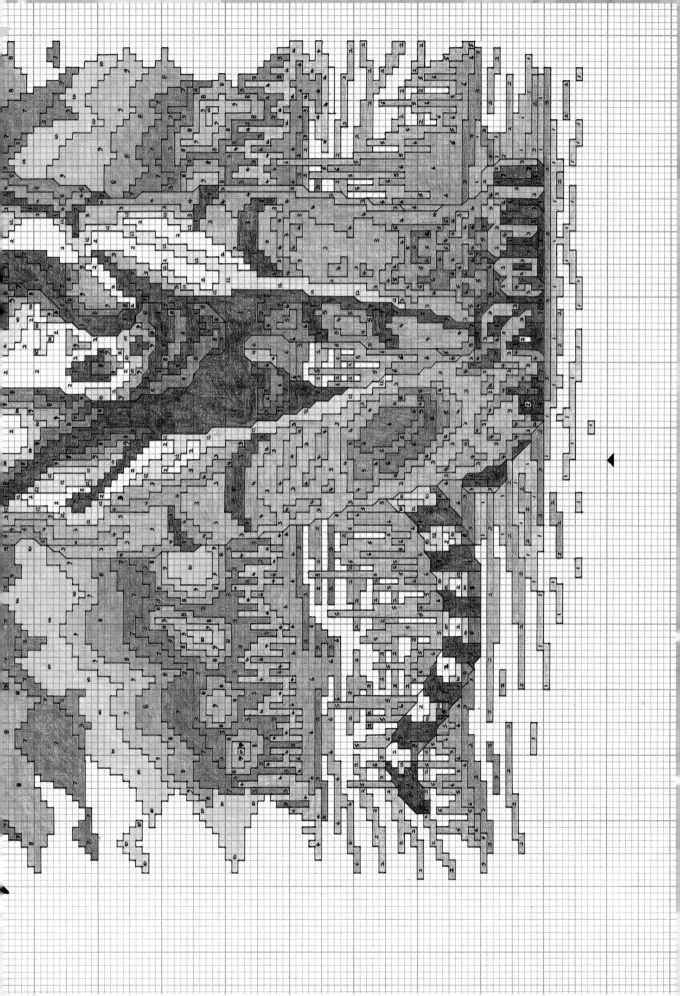

Cheetah and Cubs

At FIRST *glance, you might take this picture of a cheetah with her playful cubs reclining in the open grasslands to be a painting rather than an embroidery. It is, however, one of the biggest and most ambitious projects in the book. The great attention to detail and clever use of colour help to create a lifelike impression which would be an enjoyable challenge for any experienced needleworker.*

Finished design size: 36cm (14¼in) square approximately using Aida, 14 blocks to 2.5cm (1in)

56cm (22in) square white Aida (Zweigart E3706), 14 blocks to 2.5cm (1in)

DMC STRANDED COTTON (FLOSS)

1 skein:	ecru	light grey 3024
	grey 3023	grey 3022
	deep brown 838	dark brown 839
	mid-brown 840	mid-brown 841
	light brown 842	dark brown 898
	dark brown 3371	pale beige 677
	beige 676	buff 738
	buff 437	brown 433
	dark gold 780	dark gold 782
	gold 783	tan 976
	dark tan 975	rust 921
	dark rust 919	pale buff 739
	dark brown 3021	
2 skeins:	black 310	white
	light tan 977	

Background

1 skein:	khaki green 3053	khaki green 3052
	dark khaki green 3051	light brown 834
	light brown 833	brown 831
	mushroom 613	khaki 372
	khaki 371	dark mushroom 610
	olive green 734	olive green 733

dark olive green 732	deep olive green 730
deep brown 838	dark beige 680
brown 830	

1 Before you start stitching the design, read through Techniques on pages 8-9 to find out how to prepare your fabric, mark the centre point and start off your thread.

2 Match the tacking (basting) lines on the fabric with the arrows at the sides of the chart, and then work the design from the centre outwards. Work the cheetah and cubs first, followed by the foreground, and then background.

3 The cheetah, cubs and foreground are worked in cross stitch using two strands of stranded cotton (floss). The far background area is worked in cross stitch using one strand of stranded cotton (floss). This area is indicated by a thin broken black line on the chart.

4 Backstitch is worked using one strand of stranded cotton (floss). Work backstitch detail using white for the whiskers, dark brown 3021 around the mother's mouth and dark brown 839 around her ears. Refer to the Stitch Guide on pages 10-11 for instructions on working the stitches.

5 Refer to Mounting and Framing on page 9 for instructions on completing your picture.

CHEETAHS

*T*HE *cheetah is the fastest living land animal and can reach speeds of up to 114kmh/(70mph). They hunt by sight and rush at their prey, out-manoeuvring it through their speed and agility. Males sometimes travel in pairs, but the female lives alone. She usually gives birth to four or five cubs, but sadly about half of the cubs born alive die within the first eight months of life and only one-third of those left survive to a year old. Unlike other cats, cheetahs' eyes have round pupils, and they are unable to retract their claws.*

61

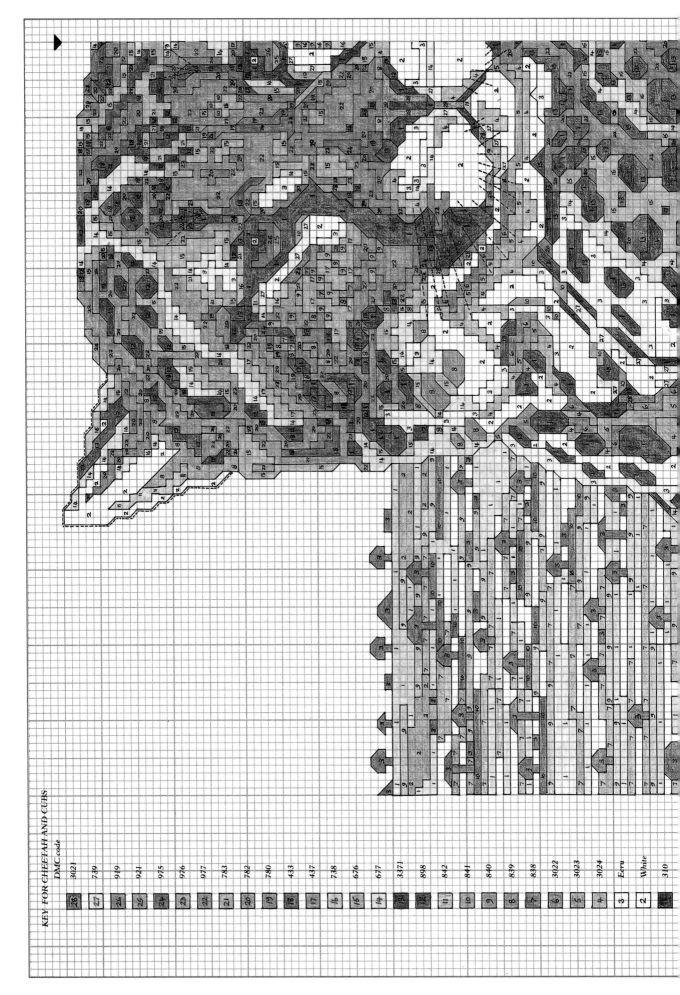

KEY FOR CHEETAH AND CUBS

	DMC code	
28	3021	
27	739	
26	919	
25	921	
24	975	
23	976	
22	977	
21	783	
20	782	
19	780	
18	433	
17	437	
16	738	
15	676	
14	677	
13	3371	
12	898	
11	842	
10	841	
9	840	
8	839	
7	838	
6	3022	
5	3023	
4	3024	
3	Ecru	
2	White	
	310	

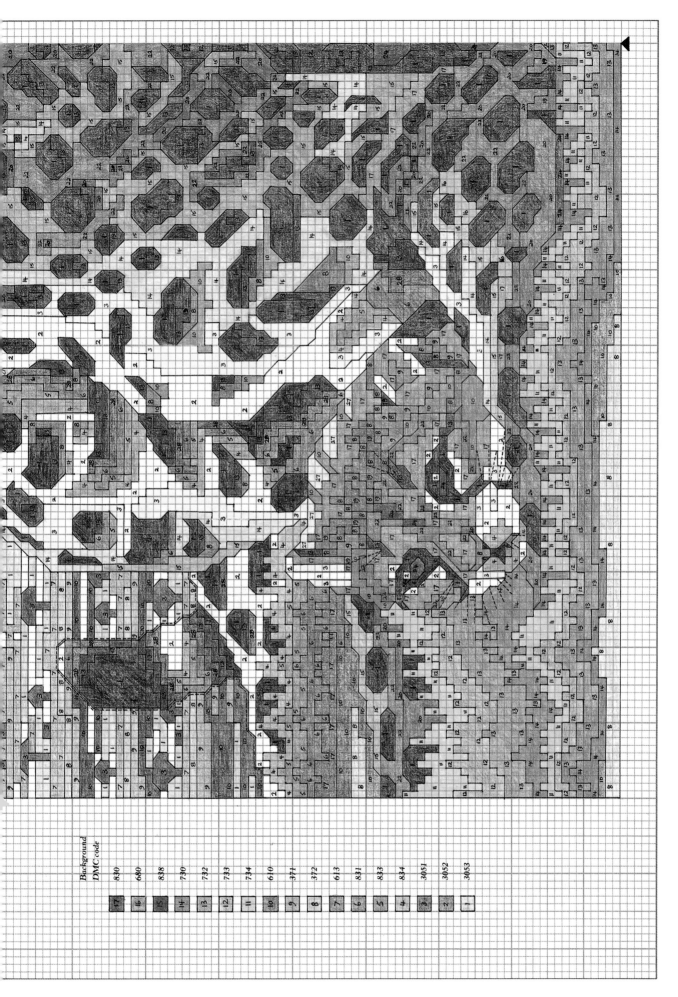

Background DMC code	
830	17
680	16
838	15
730	14
732	13
733	12
734	11
610	10
371	9
372	8
613	7
831	6
833	5
834	4
3051	3
3052	2
3053	1

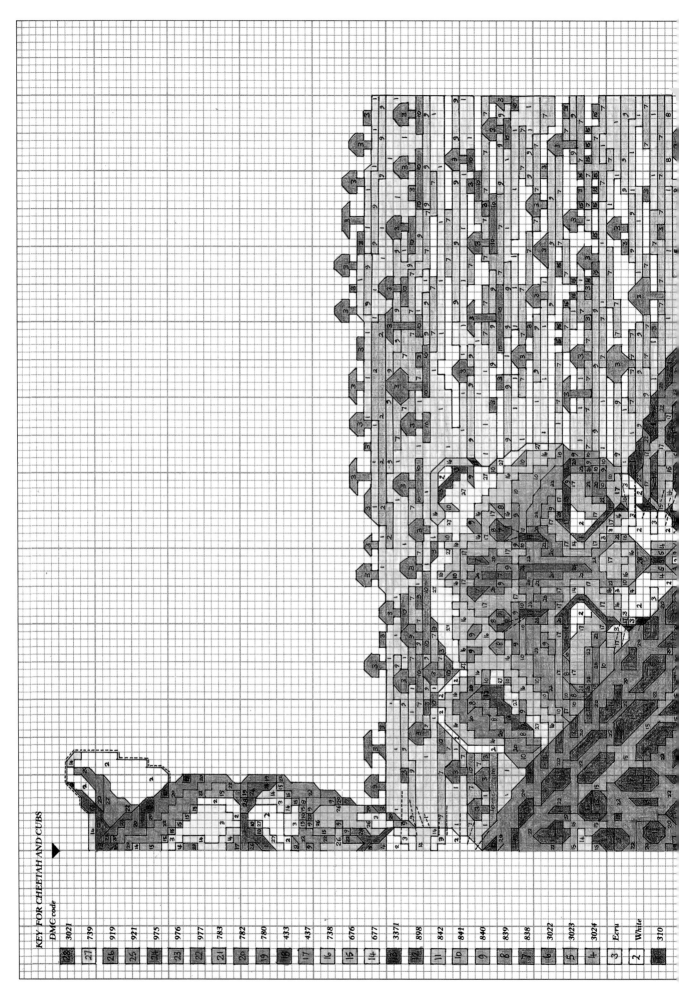

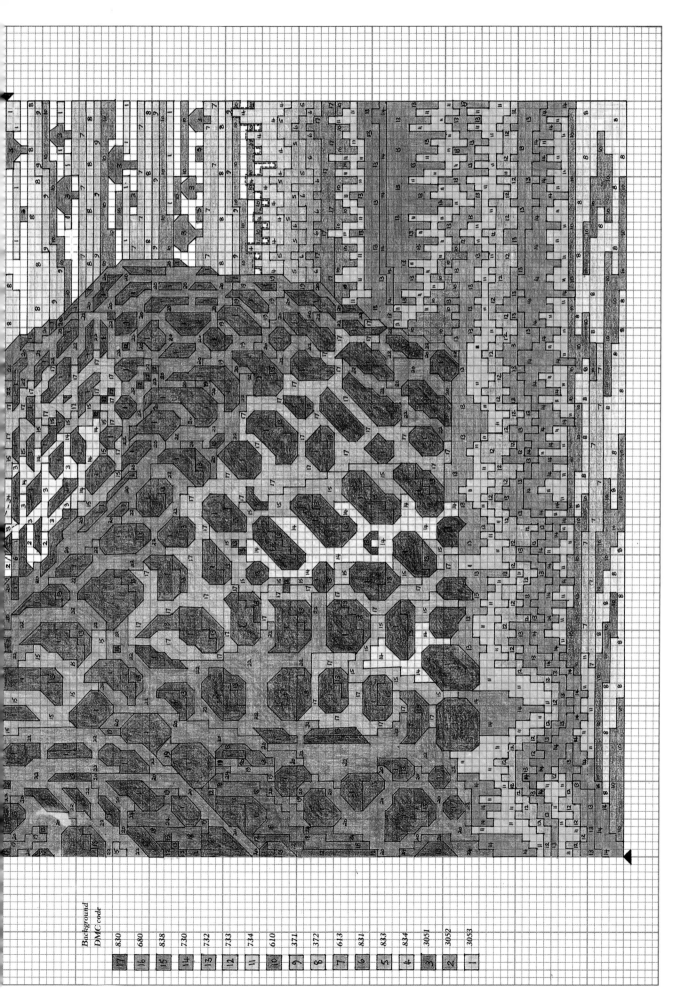

Background		
DMG code		
830	17	
680	16	
838	15	
730	14	
732	13	
733	12	
734	11	
610	10	
371	9	
372	8	
613	7	
831	6	
833	5	
834	4	
3051	3	
3052	2	
3053	1	

Beautiful Butterfly Shawl and Waistcoat

*T*HIS *elegant damask waistcoat and shawl have been beautifully decorated using the colourful orange tip butterfly design (see photograph 68). The shawl is worked on Afghan, a soft, evenweave fabric with tramlines running through it which create squares on the fabric. The waistcoat uses a patterned damask fabric which has small circles of Aida woven into it. Also included is another design of the Camberwell beauty (see photograph 69), which would look stunning worked on black fabric.*

ORANGE TIP BUTTERFLY SHAWL

Finished design size: 10cm (4in) diameter
approximately worked on Afghan (Anne)
evenweave fabric, 18 threads to 2.5cm (1in).

117cm (46in) square Anne evenweave fabric
   (Zweigart E7563), 18 threads to 2.5cm (1in)
Matching sewing thread

(contd)

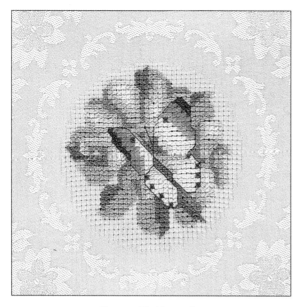

Orange Tip Butterfly

DMC STRANDED COTTON (FLOSS)

1 skein:
white	dark mushroom 610
orange 741	orange 742
beige 951	grey 453
mid-grey 451	green 3347
deep yellow 743	green 988
medium pink 962	pink 776
pale pink 963	

2 skeins: light green 3348

1 Before you start stitching the design, read through Techniques on pages 8-9 to find out how to prepare your fabric, mark the centre point and start off your thread.

2 Match the tacking (basting) lines on the fabric with the arrows at the sides of the chart, and then work the design from the centre outwards.

3 The cross stitch in this design is worked using three strands of stranded cotton (floss), and the backstitch using one strand. Refer to the Stitch Guide on pages 10-11 for instructions on working the stitches on Afghan (Anne) fabric. Work backstitch detail using dark mushroom 610 to outline the butterfly.

4 Cut the fabric so that you have 7 x 7 squares, allowing extra fabric at each edge for fringing (see step 5). The shawl has six butterflies stitched on alternate squares of one corner of the fabric. Follow the design layout shown in Fig 1, or create your own design by stitching butterflies at random.

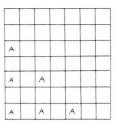

Fig 1 Design layout

5 For the fringing, make a row of machine or hand stitches about 6.5cm (2½in) in from the outer edges. Tease away the threads from each edge, stopping when you reach the row of stitches, which will prevent the fabric from fraying any further.

ORANGE TIP BUTTERFLY WAISTCOAT

Finished design size: 10cm (4in) diameter approximately worked on Schönfels, 11 blocks to 2.5cm (1in) or Aida with 11 blocks to 2.5cm (1in).

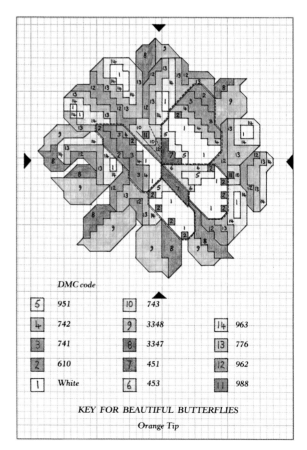

DMC code

5	951	10	743		
4	742	9	3348	14	963
3	741	8	3347	13	776
2	610	7	451	12	962
1	White	6	453	11	988

KEY FOR BEAUTIFUL BUTTERFLIES

Orange Tip

Purchased pattern for waistcoat

Schönfels damask patterned fabric (Zweigart E2144) or other linen or blockweave fabric, (refer to pattern for fabric requirements)

Plastic cover buttons (refer to pattern for number of buttons required)

Matching sewing thread

1 Follow the list of stranded cotton (floss) requirements given for the Orange Tip Butterfly Shawl, but you will only need one skein of each colour.

2 Lay the pattern pieces for the waistcoat fronts on to the fabric and tack (baste) around their shapes with sewing thread. You may find it easier to stitch the designs on to the fabric before cutting out the waistcoat fronts.

3 Follow steps 1-3 for the shawl, but when referring to the Stitch Guide, follow the instructions for working stitches on Aida fabric.

4 Make up the waistcoat following the instructions for the purchased pattern. Finish by adding covered buttons, choosing a colour to complement those used in the design. To make up the buttons, follow the manufacturer's instructions.

CAMBERWELL BEAUTY BUTTERFLY

Finished design size: 10cm (4in) diameter approximately worked on Afghan (Anne) evenweave fabric, 18 threads to 2.5cm (1in), or Schönfels damask fabric with 11 blocks to 2.5cm (1in)

DMC STRANDED COTTON (FLOSS)

1 skein:	
black 310	white
green 3346	mid-green 3364
foxglove 3607	light foxglove 3609
pale pink 818	dull red 221
dull purple 3740	dark brown 938
brown 3781	yellow 727
light blue 3755	

1 Follow steps 1 and 2 for the Orange Tip Butterfly Shawl.

2 The cross stitch in this design is worked using three strands of stranded cotton (floss) and the backstitch using one strand. When referring to the Stitch Guide on pages 10-11, note that instructions are given for working stitches on both Aida and Afghan (Anne) fabric.

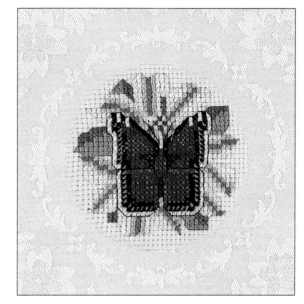

Camberwell Beauty Butterfly

3 Complete the design by working backstitch detail using black 310 to outline the butterfly, light foxglove 3609 to work around the petal edges and mid-green 3346 around the outer leaf edges.

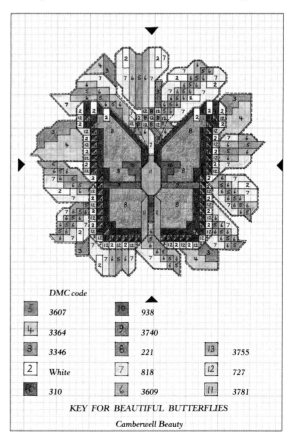

DMC code			
5 3607	10 938		
4 3364	9 3740		
3 3346	8 221	13 3755
2 White	7 818	12 727
1 310	6 3609	11 3781

KEY FOR BEAUTIFUL BUTTERFLIES

Camberwell Beauty

Garden Bird Collection

*T*HESE *lively little birds surrounded by hedgerows in full bloom were designed specially for the Garden Bird Collection. The delicate pastel cushions have been worked on a cream background, and the design is then dramatically transformed to create the canvas rug worked in tapestry yarn using vibrant colours on a rich black background (see page 78). The Summer design shows the long-tailed tit and the Autumn design the coal tit (top left), great tit (bottom left) and the blue tit (right).*

SUMMER

Finished design size: 32cm (12½in) square approximately using Aida, 14 blocks to 2.5cm (1in)

47cm (18½in) square cream Aida (Zweigart E3706), 14 blocks to 2.5cm (1in)
46cm (18in) x 115cm (45in) wide cotton chintz fabric for backing and piping
1.5m (1⅝yd) medium piping cord
25.5cm (10in) zip
Matching sewing thread
Paper for template
Square cushion pad to fit

(contd)

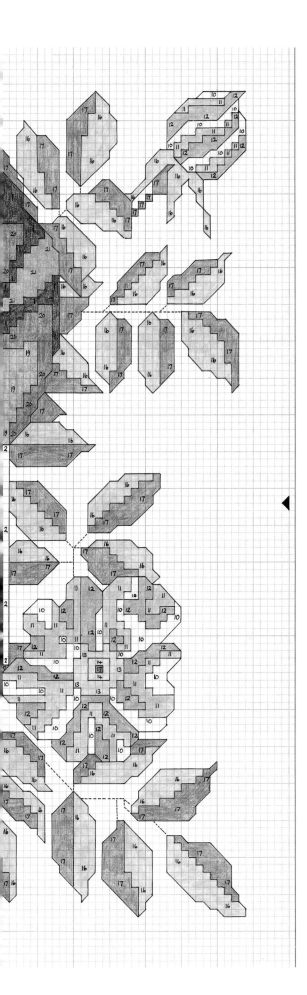

DMC STRANDED COTTON (FLOSS)

1 skein:	black 310	white
	pale pink 963	pink 3716
	medium pink 962	dark pink 961
	raspberry 3350	deep yellow 743
	blue 799	pale pink 818
	beige 676	pink 899
	green 988	mid-green 3364
	mid-grey 451	grey 453
	rose pink 758	dark grey 535
2 skeins:	pink 776	light green 3348
	green 3347	

1 Before you start stitching the design, read through Techniques on pages 8-9 to find out how to prepare your fabric, mark the centre point and start off your thread.

2 Match the tacking (basting) lines on the fabric with the arrows at the sides of the chart, and then work the design from the centre outwards, finishing with the border. When working the border, repeat Chart 1 (pages 76-7) four times, matching the diagonal edges at each end to complete the corner flower.

3 The cross stitch and backstitch in this design are both worked using two strands of stranded cotton (floss). Refer to the Stitch Guide on pages 10-11 for instructions on working the stitches. Work backstitch detail using green 3347 for the leaf stalks.

4 To make the ruched piping for the cushion,

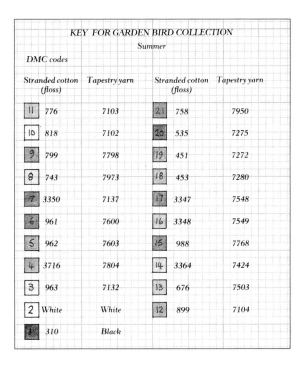

KEY FOR GARDEN BIRD COLLECTION
Summer

DMC codes

Stranded cotton (floss)	Tapestry yarn	Stranded cotton (floss)	Tapestry yarn
11 776	7103	21 758	7950
10 818	7102	20 535	7275
9 799	7798	19 451	7272
8 743	7973	18 453	7280
7 3350	7137	17 3347	7548
6 961	7600	16 3348	7549
5 962	7603	15 988	7768
4 3716	7804	14 3364	7424
3 963	7132	13 676	7503
2 White	White	12 899	7104
1 310	Black		

follow the instructions for the Humming-bird Cushion given on pages 45-7. To make up the cushion, follow steps 1, 2, 3 and 5 of the making-up instructions for the Siamese Cat Cushion given on page 14.

AUTUMN

Finished design size: 32cm (12½in) square approximately using Aida, 14 blocks to 2.5cm (1in)

47cm (18½in) square cream Aida (Zweigart E3706), 14 blocks to 2.5cm (1in)
46cm (18in) x 115cm (45in) wide cotton chintz fabric for backing and piping
1.5m (1⅝yd) medium piping cord
25.5cm (10in) zip
Matching sewing thread
Paper for template
Square cushion pad to fit

DMC STRANDED COTTON (FLOSS)
1 skein: black 310   white
           dark blue 930   airforce blue 931
           mid-blue 932   dark khaki green 3051
           khaki green 3052   pale yellow 744
           pale yellow 745   mid-grey 451
           dark grey 535   beige 951
           dark gold 782   light green 3348
           green 3347   dark brown 801
           red 321   red 606
           deep orange 608   grey 453

KEY FOR GARDEN BIRD COLLECTION			
Autumn			
DMC codes			
Stranded cotton (floss)	Tapestry yarn	Stranded cotton (floss)	Tapestry yarn
10 451	7272	20 453	7280
9 745	7078	19 608	7946
8 744	7727	18 606	7606
7 3052	7426	17 321	7544
6 3051	7377	16 801	7468
5 932	7593	15 3347	7548
4 931	7695	14 3348	7549
3 930	7930	13 782	7782
2 White	White	12 951	7171
1 310	Black	11 535	7275

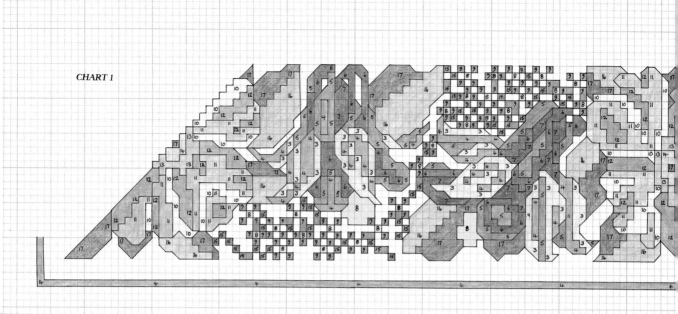

CHART 1

GARDEN BIRDS

*T*HE long tail helps the agile little long-tailed tit keep its balance during flight or when hedge hopping in search of food. In spring, the birds build unusual ball-shaped nests, covered with moss and lined with feathers, and usually placed in the fork of a tree or bush, or hanging in brambles.

The coal tit sometimes feasts at birdtables, but generally feeds from tree bark on a diet of insects, spiders and grubs. Nests lined with animal hair, rabbit fur and feathers are built in spring in old tree stumps, rabbit burrows or in the foundations of larger nests.

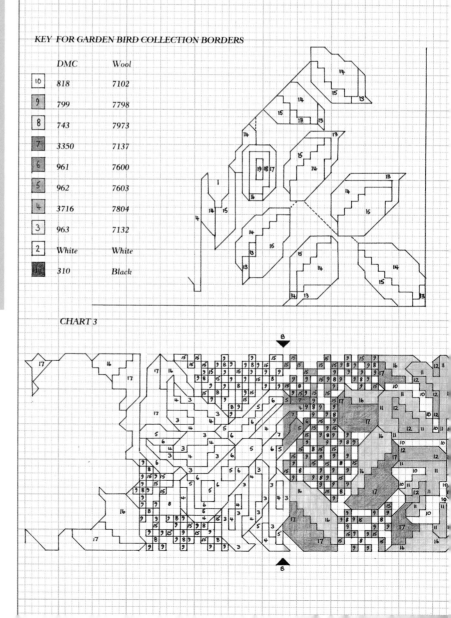

CHART 2

KEY FOR GARDEN BIRD COLLECTION BORDERS

	DMC	Wool
10	818	7102
9	799	7798
8	743	7973
7	3350	7137
6	961	7600
5	962	7603
4	3716	7804
3	963	7132
2	White	White
	310	Black

CHART 3

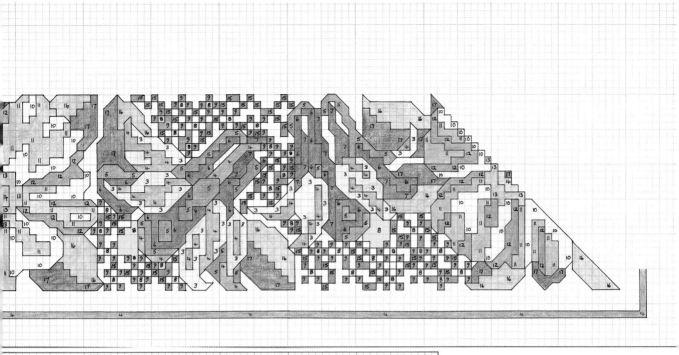

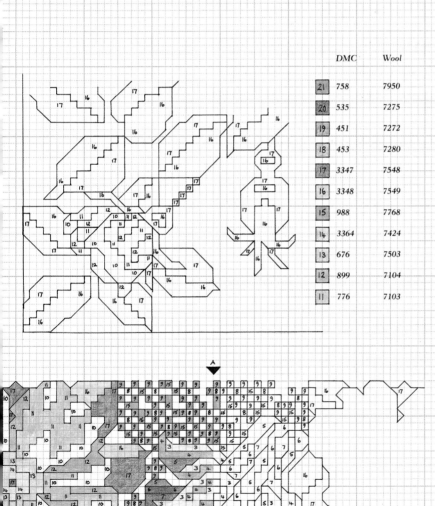

	DMC	Wool
21	758	7950
20	535	7275
19	451	7272
18	453	7280
17	3347	7548
16	3348	7549
15	988	7768
14	3364	7424
13	676	7503
12	899	7104
11	776	7103

GARDEN BIRDS

*T*HE great tit is the largest member of the family. It lives on a varied diet of insects, beetles, bees, worms, nuts and buds, but also is notorious for stealing the cream from milk bottles. Nests are built in spring in tree stumps, nestboxes and odd places such as flowerpots and windowboxes.

Finally, the blue tit is a colourful little acrobat and the most popular and widely distributed member of the family. It visits birdtables freely to feed on coconut, suet and nuts. Nests are built in or near houses, in stone walls, holes in trees, nestboxes, gateposts, water pumps and in hedgerows.

1 Before you start stitching the design, read through Techniques on pages 8-9 to find out how to prepare your fabric, mark the centre point and start off your thread.

2 Match the tacking (basting) lines on the fabric with the arrows at the sides of the chart, and then work the design from the centre outwards, finishing with the border. When working the border, repeat Chart 1 four times, matching the diagonal edges at each end to complete the corner flower.

3 The cross stitch and backstitch in this design are both worked using two strands of stranded cotton (floss). Refer to the Stitch Guide on pages 10-11 for instructions on working the stitches. Work backstitch detail using green 3347 for the leaf stalks.

4 To make the ruched piping for the cushion, follow the instructions for the Humming-bird Cushion given on pages 45-7. To make up the cushion, follow steps 1, 2, 3 and 5 of the making-up instructions for the Siamese Cat Cushion given on page 14.

GARDEN BIRD RUG

This beautiful rug with its bright colours, rich borders and dark background has been worked using tapestry yarn on canvas. Brighter colours have been used than those for the cushions, to add vibrancy to the design. You will need to follow the charts for the Summer and Autumn designs together with Charts 1, 2 and 3 to create the pretty hedgerow border which runs around the outer edge. Shade codes for both DMC stranded cotton (floss) and tapestry yarn are listed in the keys at the side of each chart.

Finished design size: 67 x 108cm (26½in x 42½in) using a rug canvas, 7 holes to 2.5cm (1in).

81 x 122cm (32 x 48in), ecru Sudan Canvas (Zweigart E699) 7 holes to 2.5cm (1in)
Large tapestry frame
Tapestry needle
Thimble

DMC TAPESTRY YARN 8m (8¼yd) SKEINS

1 skein:	beige 7950	grey 7272
	light green 7424	dark blue 7930
	dark blue 7695	blue 7593
	dark green 7377	dark green 7426

DMC TAPESTRY YARN

	yellow 7727	dark lemon 7078
	dark cream 7171	dark brown 7468
	deep orange 7606	orange 7946
2 skeins:	white	dark grey 7275
	light grey 7280	pale green 7503
	rust 7782	red 7544
3 skeins:	green 7768	bright yellow 7973
	deep cerise 7137	
4 skeins:	cornflower blue 7798	cerise 7600
5 skeins:	dark pink 7603	
6 skeins:	dark salmon 7104	pale pink 7132
7 skeins:	light salmon 7102	pink 7804
9 skeins:	salmon 7103	
17 skeins:	light green 7549	
23 skeins:	green 7548	
15 x 38m (41½yd) skeins: black		

1 Prepare the canvas by measuring a 7.5cm (3in) hem at each edge, then mark the hem lines with tacking (basting) stitches. This line will help to position the stitching centrally on the canvas and give you the approximate size of the rug.

2 Rug canvas tends to stretch and lose its shape easily. To prevent this and to make working easier, mount the work on to a large frame. To work the stitches, use a large tapestry needle with a blunt end and a large eye through which to thread the yarn. As stitching may become quite tough, use a thimble to protect your fingers.

3 The cross stitch and backstitch in this design are both worked using one strand of tapestry yarn. Refer to the Stitch Guide on pages 10-11 for instructions on how to work the stitches. For three-quarter cross stitch, the shorter diagonal stitch is worked by inserting the needle directly into the canvas by splitting the mesh. If you find this too difficult, replace these stitches with a half cross stitch (refer to Stitch Guide).

4 Follow Chart 1 to stitch one short border strip, then stitch the long border strips by following Chart 1 and then Chart 3, which shows the border extension. Match up the diagonal edges at each end to complete the corner flower. Next, work from the right-hand corner to point A, or from the left-hand corner to point B. These points are marked by arrows and letters on each chart. Points A and B on Chart 1 match up with points A and B on Chart 3.

5 When working on the border extensions, refer to Fig 1. Follow Chart 1 and stitch from the right-hand corner to point A, then follow Chart 3 and work from point A to B. To finish the long side, match point B on Chart 1 to point B on Chart 3.

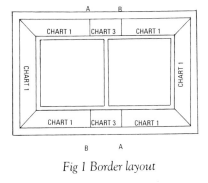

Fig 1 Border layout

Follow Chart 1 and work from point B to the left-hand corner. Chart 2 shows how to match up the sections at points A and B. Repeat for the other long side, then work the final short border.

6 When the hedgerow border is complete, work seven rows of cross stitch in black to form a band all around the inner edge of the border and across the centre. Then work the Summer and Autumn designs to complete the central panel.

7 Stitch the outer border by working three rows of cross stitch in black, one row in pink 7804 and two rows in black (see Chart 1). Finally, overcast the outer edges using green 7548. To do this, fold the canvas turnings to the back of the rug, leaving one hole showing and one thread running across the top of the fold. Stitch the turnings in place.

8 To work the overcast edging, secure the thread at the back of the canvas, insert the needle into the second hole down from the folded edge and pull to the front of the canvas. The overcast thread should share a hole with the last stitch of the cross stitch border. Take the needle to the back of the canvas and work the next stitch in the same way (Fig 2). Work two or three stitches in each hole to cover the canvas completely.

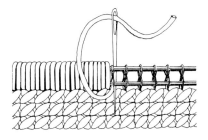

Fig 2 Working overcast edging

Dragonflies and Damselflies Table Linen

*B*RIGHTLY *coloured dragonflies and delicate damselflies decorate this elegant collection of table linen, coasters and jam-pot covers. The tablecloth centre has fragile dragonflies fluttering amongst the small pink flowers of the flowering rush, with small sprigs of foliage to decorate each corner. Single insects are repeated on the tray cloth, napkins with matching napkin rings, coasters and jam-pot covers. These versatile little designs could be used for any small needlework projects.*

DRAGONFLY TABLECLOTH

Finished design size: 26cm (10¼in) square
approximately using Aida, 14 blocks to 2.5cm (1in)

1.1m (1¼yd) square, white Aida (Zweigart E3706), 14 blocks to 2.5cm (1in)
Matching sewing thread

(contd page 84)

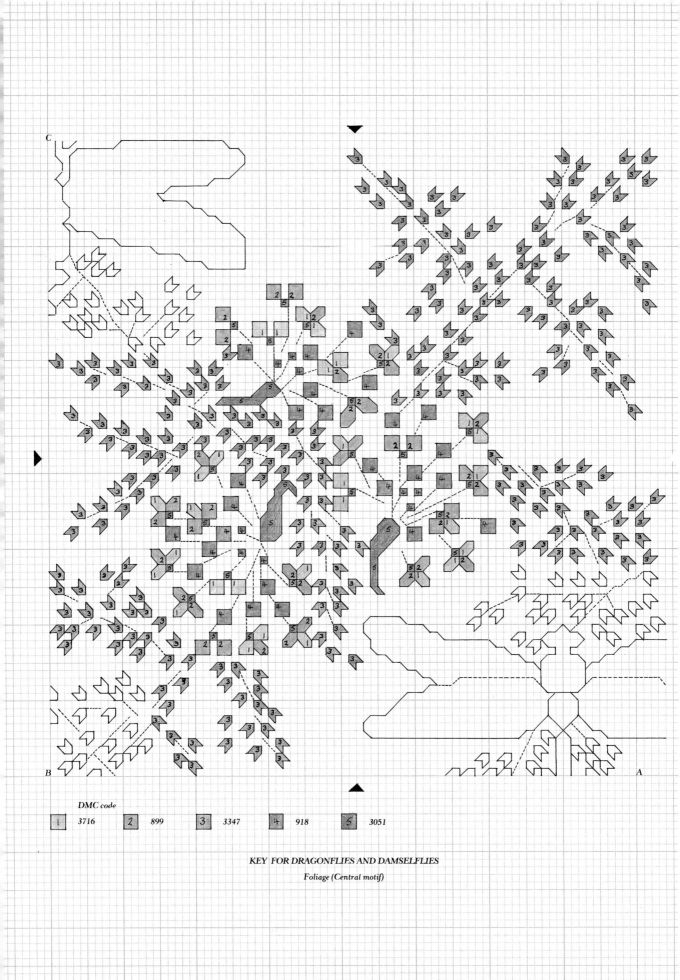

KEY FOR DRAGONFLIES AND DAMSELFLIES

Foliage (Central motif)

DMC code

| 1 | 3716 | 2 | 899 | 3 | 3347 | 4 | 918 | 5 | 3051 |

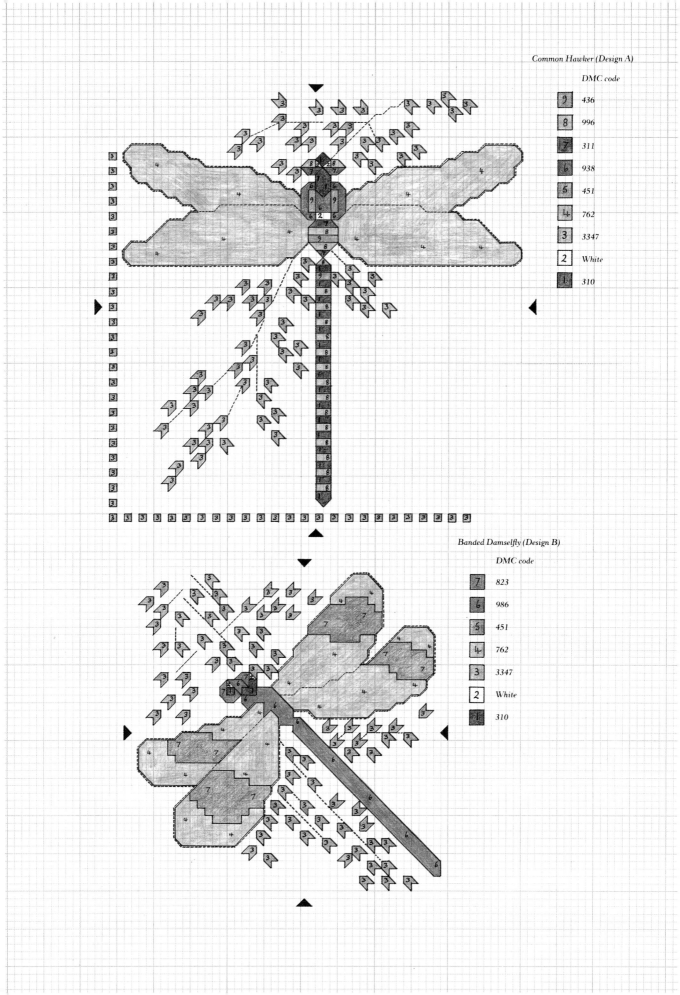

Common Hawker (Design A)

DMC code

9	436
8	996
7	311
6	938
5	451
4	762
3	3347
2	White
1	310

Banded Damselfly (Design B)

DMC code

7	823
6	986
5	451
4	762
3	3347
2	White
1	310

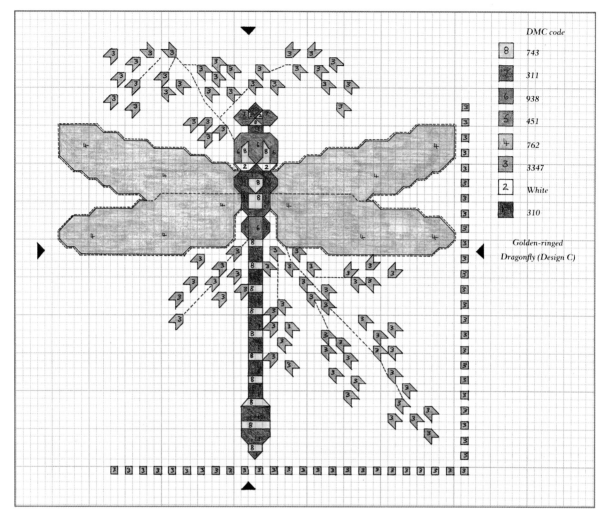

DMC code	
8	*743*
7	*311*
6	*938*
5	*451*
4	*762*
3	*3347*
2	*White*
	310

Golden-ringed
Dragonfly (Design C)

DMC STRANDED COTTON (FLOSS)

Foliage

1 skein	pink 3716	pink 899
	green 3347	dark rust 918
	dark khaki green 3051	

Common hawker (design A)

1 skein	black 310	white
	green 3347	light grey 762
	mid-grey 451	buff 938
	dark blue 311	turquoise 996
	dark buff 436	

Banded damselfly (design B)

1 skein:	black 310	white
	green 3347	light grey 762
	mid-grey 451	dark green 986
	navy blue 823	

Golden-ringed dragonfly (design C)

1 skein:	black 310	white
	green 3347	light grey 762
	mid-grey 451	buff 938
	dark blue 311	deep yellow 743

1 Before you start stitching the design, read through Techniques on pages 8-9 to find out how to prepare your fabric, mark the centre point and start off your thread.

2 Match the tacking (basting) lines on the fabric with the arrows at the sides of the chart, and then work the design from the centre outwards.

3 The cross stitch in this design is worked using two strands of stranded cotton (floss) and the backstitch using one strand. Refer to the Stitch Guide on pages 10-11 for instructions on working the stitches. Work backstitch detail using green 3347 for the foliage stems, and mid-grey 451 to outline the insects' wings.

4 Neaten the raw edges of the cloth by pressing up a 1.5cm (⅝in) turning, and then stitch the hem in place. You could make a decorative hem by hand embroidering if you wish.

5 Follow the chart to work up the foliage for the

centre motif. The placement of each insect is indicated on the chart with the letters A, B and C, which correspond to the separate design charts. An outline of the wing-tip shapes has been shown as a thin black line.

6 Work a small floral motif at each corner, 2.5cm (1in) from the hemmed edges. To finish, work two rows of cross stitches to form a border along the outer edges of each corner motif. For each row, work 25 cross stitches on alternate blocks, four blocks down from the motif (see photograph on pages 80-1).

DAMSELFLY NAPKIN RINGS AND COASTERS (4)

Finished design size: 5cm (2in) square approximately using Oslo, 22 blocks to 2.5cm (1in)

For the napkin rings: 20 x 36cm (7¾ x 14¼in) white Oslo (Zweigart E3947), 22 blocks to 2.5cm (1in)
20 x 36cm (7¾in x 14¼in) matching cotton for backing fabric
104cm (40in) green satin ribbon
For the coasters: 28cm (11in) square white Oslo (Zweigart E3947), 22 blocks to 2.5cm (1in)
4 purchased coasters for needlework

1 Follow the stranded cotton (floss) requirements given for the Dragonfly Tablecloth, design B. Then follow steps 1, 2 and 3.
2 Work the designs by following Chart B. Cut rectangles from the stitched fabric and backing fabric, measuring 8 x 20cm (3 x 7¾in) for each ring. Press a 6mm (¼in) turning all round.
3 With wrong sides facing, pin rectangles of the two fabrics together, so that the turnings are concealed. Cut the green satin ribbon into 13cm (5in) lengths, then pin a length of ribbon at each short end, sandwiched between both layers, and then stitch all layers together. Use the satin ribbons to tie each strip into a ring.
4 The coasters use the same fabric and design as the napkin rings. To mount the finished work, follow the manufacturer's instructions.
5 The damselfly jam-pot covers use the same design as the napkin rings. Work your design on the fabric, then cut a circle of fabric to the required size. Finish the jampot cover by adding a pretty lace trim around the edge.

DRAGONFLY NAPKINS (4)

Finished design size: 6.5cm (2½in) square approximately using Oslo, 22 blocks to 2.5cm (1in)

For each napkin: 33cm (13in) square white Oslo (Zweigart E3947), 22 blocks to 2.5cm (1in)
Matching sewing thread

1 Follow the list of stranded cotton (floss) requirements given for the Dragonfly Tablecloth, designs A and C. Then follow steps 1, 2 and 3.
2 Neaten the raw edges of each napkin by pressing up a 1cm (½in) turning, and then stitch the hem in place. You could make a decorative hem by hand embroidering if you wish.
3 Work design A at the lower left corner of two napkins and design C at the lower right corner of the remaining two napkins, 4.5cm (1¾in) from the hemmed edges.
4 Finish by using green 3347 to work a border along the two outer edges of each design by working two rows of 25 cross stitches on alternate blocks. For the fringed edge, follow the instructions for the Dragonfly Tray Cloth, step 4.

DRAGONFLY TRAY CLOTH

Finished design size: 10cm (4in) square approximately using Aida, 14 blocks to 2.5cm (1in)

30 x 40.5cm (12 x 16in) white Aida (Zweigart E3706), 14 blocks to 2.5cm (1in)
Matching sewing thread

1 Follow the list of stranded cotton (floss) requirements given for the Dragonfly Tablecloth, designs A and C. Then follow steps 1, 2 and 3.
2 Work design A at the lower left corner of one short edge, and design C at the opposite right corner of one long edge of the cloth. The head of each dragonfly should face towards the centre.
3 Work a border using green 3347 along the two outer edges of each design by working two rows of 25 cross stitches on alternate blocks. Then work a border of alternate cross stitches 2.5cm (1in) from the outer edge.
4 For the fringed edge, run a row of machine stitches close to the cross stitch border and then tease away the threads. The machine stitches prevent the fabric fraying further.

Thomas Cat

*T*HIS *rather smart black-and-white cat is called Thomas and is one of the many animals that live with Jayne in her small country cottage. Although he is black and white, many different shades of grey, cream and beige have been used to make him appear so lifelike. The design is worked in cross stitch and three-quarter cross stitch, with long backstitches being used to add the whisker detail. The parchment-coloured Aida provides a superb background setting.*

Finished design size: 19 x 34cm (7½ x 13½in) approximately using Aida, 14 blocks to 2.5cm (1in).

33 x 51cm (13 x 20in) parchment Aida (Zweigart E3706), 14 blocks to 2.5cm (1in)

DMC STRANDED COTTON (FLOSS)

1 skein:	grey 414	grey 318
	mid-grey 415	light grey 762
	dark rose pink 356	rose pink 758
	dark mushroom 640	mushroom 642
	light mushroom 644	pale mushroom 822
	dark beige 3045	beige 3046
	pale yellow 744	pale lemon 3078
	cream 746	flesh 948
2 skeins:	black 310	white
	darkest grey 413	grey 317

Background

1 skein:	khaki green 3053	dark olive green 732
	olive green 734	light moss green 471
	moss green 469	dark moss green 936
	dark moss green 935	deep moss green 934
	dark mushroom 640	pale mushroom 822

1 Before you start stitching the design, read through Techniques on pages 8-9 to find out how to prepare your fabric, mark the centre point and start off your thread.

2 Match the tacking (basting) lines on the fabric with the arrows at the sides of the chart, and then work the design from the centre outwards.

3 The cross stitch in this design is worked using two strands of stranded cotton (floss). Work the whiskers with long backstitches using one strand of white stranded cotton (floss). Refer to the Stitch Guide on pages 10-11 for instructions on working the stitches.

4 Refer to Mounting and Framing on page 9 for instructions on completing your picture.

DOMESTIC CATS

*O*NE *in five households in Britain has a domestic cat or moggy, making a total of 4.8 million cats! It is thought that cats were first domesticated by the Egyptians many thousands of years ago. Phoenician travellers then introduced cats to many parts of the world, but the Romans were responsible for introducing them to Britain. Today, the domestic cat is a popular pet which is found in abundance worldwide.*

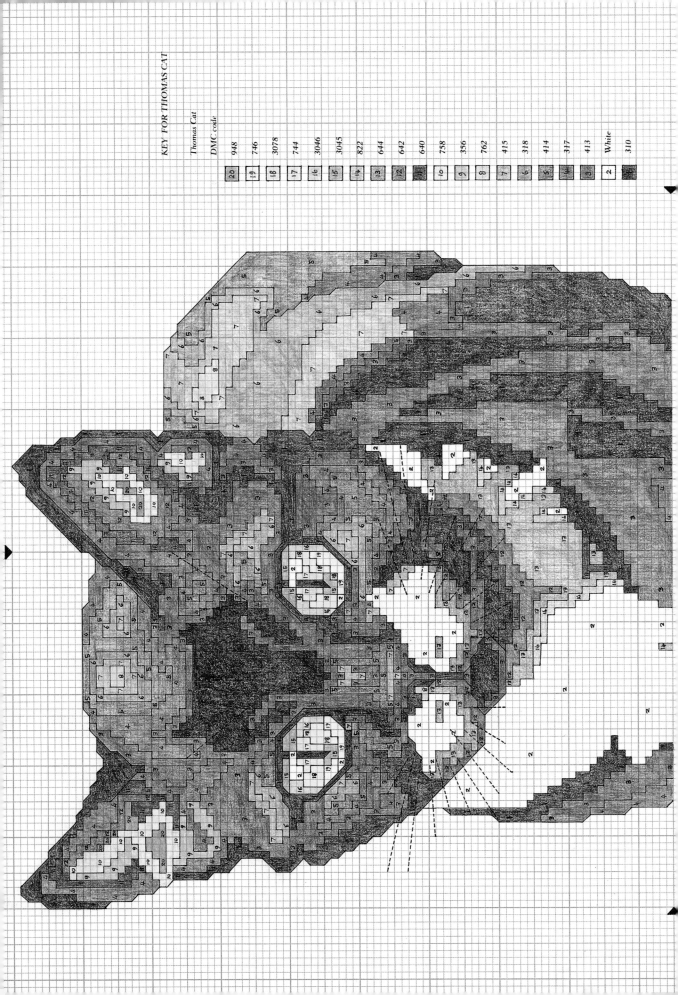

KEY FOR THOMAS CAT

Thomas Cat
DMC code

Code	DMC
20	948
19	746
18	3078
17	744
16	3046
15	3045
14	822
13	644
12	642
11	640
10	758
9	356
8	762
7	415
6	318
5	414
4	317
3	413
2	White
	310

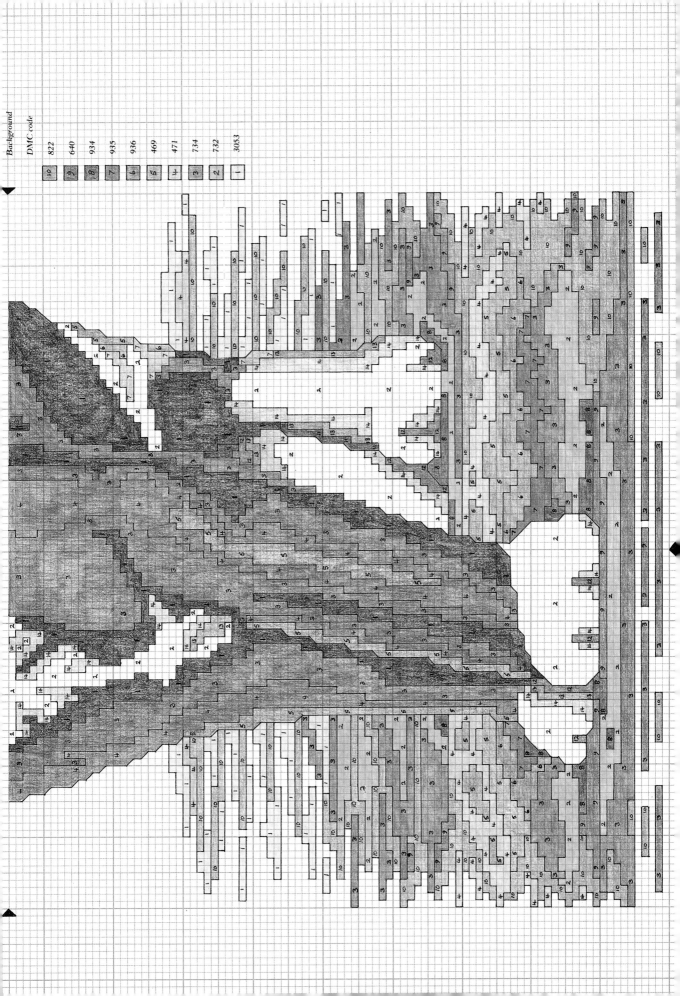

Colourful Cockerel

*T*HIS *lively cockerel makes a colourful companion to the woodland pheasant on page 95. The rich red, orange, rust and yellow colouring of the body plumage provides a warm contrast to the grey tail feathers, and backstitch has been used to add detail and definition to both. The fiery cockerel is placed amongst delicate gold foliage, which is worked using backstitch and tiny gold and coloured glass beads to add excitement and texture to the design.*

Finished design size: 27 x 30cm (10¾ x 12in) approximately using Aida, 14 blocks to 2.5cm (1in)

43 x 46cm (17 x 18in) cream Aida (Zweigart E3706), 14 blocks to 2.5cm (1in)
One small pack of tiny gold glass beads
Selection of tiny coloured glass beads

DMC STRANDED COTTON (FLOSS)

1 skein:		
	black 310	white
	red 606	deep yellow 743
	rust 921	dark copper 300
	pale buff 739	orange 741
	buff 437	deep buff 435
	dark brown 938	dark brown 3021
	darkest grey 3799	dark grey 413
	grey 317	grey 414
	grey 318	light grey 415
	light grey 762	deep navy blue 939
	deep moss green 934	light brown 3782

COCKERELS

*T*HESE *can be found worldwide on farms or in zoos and aviaries with other ornamental fowl. The Romans bred them for their decorative value and for food, but were also responsible for introducing the savage sport of cockfighting, which unfortunately still goes on today in many parts of the world. Cockerels can all be traced back to the red jungle fowl, which is still wild in parts of Asia. Cockerels are used in many parts of the world to provide feathers for bedding, arrows, darts and fashion ornaments.*

1 Before you start stitching the design, read through Techniques on pages 8-9 to find out how to prepare your fabric, mark the centre point and start off your thread.
2 Match the tacking (basting) lines on the fabric with the arrows at the sides of the chart, and then work the design from the centre outwards.
3 The cross stitch in this design is worked using two strands of stranded cotton (floss). The number of threads used for backstitch detail vary (see opposite). Refer to the Stitch Guide on pages

10-11 for instructions on working the stitches and attaching beads.

4 Work backstitch detail using two strands of stranded cotton (floss) in white for the highlights behind the eye, long pale tail feathers and tail feathers. Use one strand of stranded cotton (floss) in dark copper 300 for the head, neck, back, bottom, eye and beak areas, deep buff 435 for the yellow wing feather, black 310 for tail feathers, grey 318 for pale tail feathers and buff 437 for grass and to attach beads. Finally, use one strand of deep buff 435 to add detail to the cow parsley and the cockerel's legs, and to attach the remaining beads.

5 Refer to Mounting and Framing on page 9 for instructions on completing your picture.

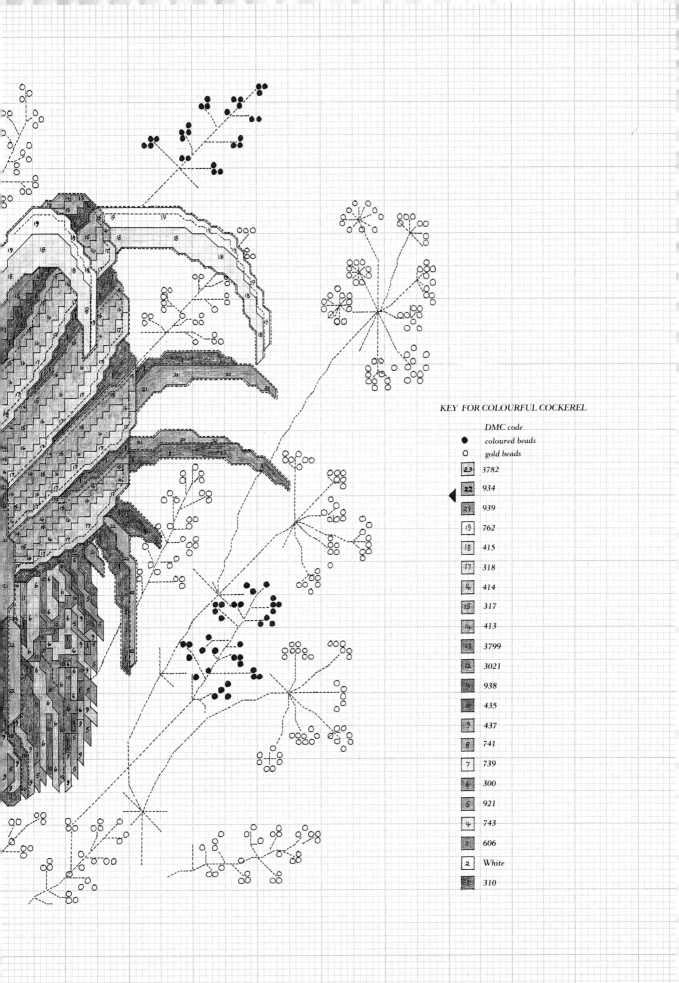

KEY FOR COLOURFUL COCKEREL

DMC code

● coloured beads
○ gold beads

23	3782
22	934
21	939
19	762
18	415
17	318
16	414
15	317
14	413
13	3799
12	3021
11	938
10	435
9	437
8	741
7	739
6	300
5	921
4	743
3	606
2	White
1	310

Woodland Pheasant

*T*HIS *is the largest and most ambitious project in the book and
should only be attempted by experienced needleworkers.
The intricate detail is achieved by the skilled use of colour and
decorative stitches. This clever combination helps to create a
magnificent picture of the male pheasant with his striking plumage,
striding through the woodland foliage.*

Finished design size: 40.5cm (16in) square
approximately using Aida, 14 blocks to 2.5cm
(1in)

51cm (20in) square white Aida (Zweigart E3706),
    14 blocks to 2.5cm (1in)

DMC STRANDED COTTON (FLOSS)

1 skein:	white	red 606
	dark green 986	light emerald green
	blue 826	703
	dark rust 918	rust 720
	orange 741	gold 783
	deep yellow 743	brown 434
	yellow 727	buff 437
	dark copper 300	dark brown 898
	beige 951	mid-brown 841
	grey 3023	dark gold 781
	buff 738	deep rose pink 3777
	orange 742	emerald green 701
	dark gold 782	light gold 725
	dark mushroom 611	mushroom 613
	dark rust 919	light emerald green
	lime green 704	703
	green 989	dark moss green 935
	sage green 523	
2 skeins:	black 310	green 988
	dark green 987	

1 Before you start stitching the design, read
through Techniques on pages 8-9 to find out how
to prepare your fabric, mark the centre point and
start off your thread.
2 Match the tacking (basting) lines on the fabric
with the arrows at the sides of the chart, and then
work the design from the centre outwards.
3 The cross stitch in this design is worked using
two strands of stranded cotton (floss). The
number of threads used for backstitch detail vary
(see opposite). Refer to the Stitch Guide on pages
10-11 for instructions on working the stitches.

PHEASANTS

*O*RIGINATING *in Asia, pheasants can now be found
virtually all over the world and are the best
known of all game birds. Although they are strong fliers,
this is limited to short bursts when escaping from pre-
dators. Only the male has the beautiful colouring, with
a dark green head, coppery underparts, white collar and
exaggerated tail feathers, whilst the female is a dull
mottled brown. They live and nest on the ground, feed-
ing on seeds, fruits, roots, berries and insects.*

4 Work backstitch detail with two strands of stranded cotton (floss) in white for the wing feathers, arrow feather markings and ladybird, dark green 986 for the stripe markings at the base of the neck, dark green 987 for the moss areas, dark brown 898 for the toadstools and finally brown 434 for the beak.

5 Work backstitch detail with one strand of stranded cotton (floss) in black 310 around the eye, red eye patch, neck, edge of tail and leg feathers, leg markings and tree stumps, use dark brown 898 for the bramble leaf veins and shoulder feathers, sage green 523 for the grass stems, white for the centre line of the tail feather and finally black 310 for the small dots on the ladybird.

6 Refer to Mounting and Framing on page 9 for instructions on completing your picture.

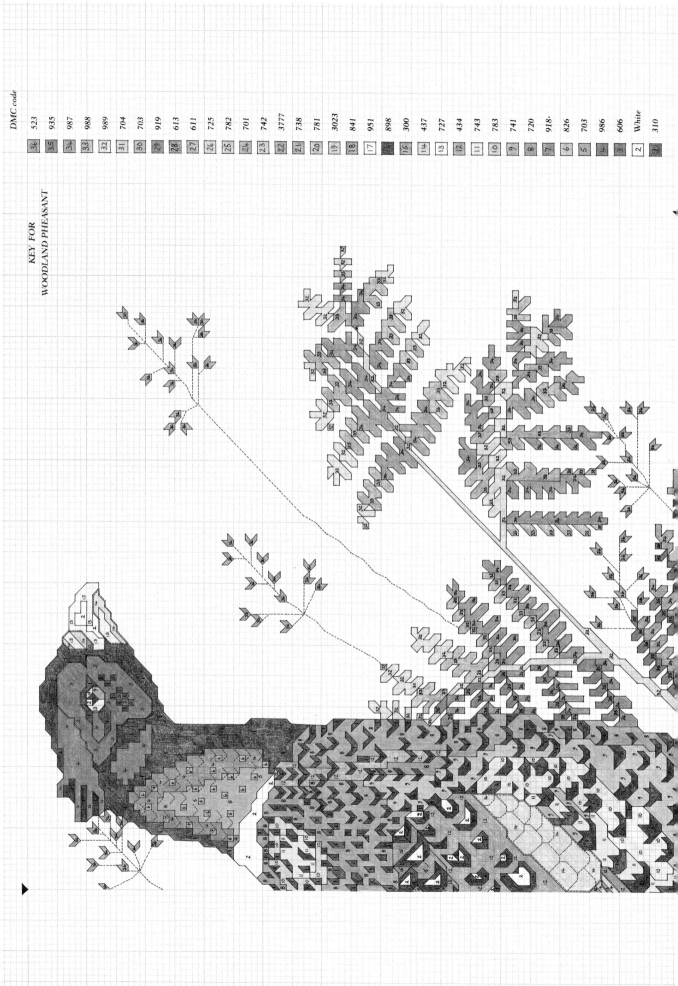

Peacocks and Doves Evening Bag and Trinkets

*E*XOTIC *peacocks inspire this classic collection of designs which has been used to decorate a trinket box, cards, sumptuous evening bag and pendant. The brightly coloured threads capture the decorative splendour of the magnificent peacock, with his wiry head crest, iridescent plumage and spectacular train adorned with eyespots. In contrast, the circular design of the graceful turtle doves flying amongst ribbons and foliage uses much softer and more subtle colouring.*

LARGE PEACOCK

Finished design size: 5cm (2in) diameter
approximately using Aida, 14 blocks to 2.5cm
(1in)

15cm (6in) square of white Aida (Zweigart E3706),
14 blocks to 2.5cm (1in)

(contd)

DMC STRANDED COTTON (FLOSS)

1 skein:	black 310	white
	lime green 907	dark blue 311
	dark blue 824	dark aqua 943
	lime green 906	dark green 991
	moss green 469	

1 Before you start stitching the design, read through Techniques on pages 8-9 to find out how to prepare your fabric, mark the centre point and start off your thread.

2 Match the tacking (basting) lines on the fabric with the arrows at the sides of the chart, and then work the design from the centre outwards.

3 The cross stitch in this design is worked using two strands of stranded cotton (floss), and the backstitch using one strand. Refer to the Stitch Guide on pages 10-11 for instructions on working the stitches. Work backstitch detail using black 310 all around the body, legs, head and crest.

4 Refer to Mounting and Framing on page 9 for instructions on completing your handbag mirror, or alternatively, a paper weight or trinket box.

SMALL PEACOCK

Finished design size: 3cm (1¼in) in diameter approximately using Lugana evenweave fabric, 25 threads to 2.5cm (1in)

15cm (6in) square of black Lugana (Zweigart E3835), 25 threads to 2.5cm (1in)
1 reel (spool) very fine metallic gold sewing thread

1 Follow the list of stranded cotton (floss) requirements given for the Large Peacock.

2 Follow steps 1 and 2 for the Large Peacock.

3 The cross stitch and backstitch in this design are both worked using one strand of stranded cotton (floss). Refer to the Stitch Guide on pages 10-11 for instructions on working the stitches. Work backstitch detail using white for the peacock legs.

4 Use the metallic gold thread to replace the black eyes of the peacock feathers and add extra sparkle.

5 Refer to Mounting and Framing on page 9 for instructions on completing your pendant, or alternatively, a trinket box or keyring.

DOVES TRINKETS

Finished design size: 7cm (2¾in) diameter approximately using Aida, 14 blocks to 2.5cm (1in)

For paperweight and greetings card: 15cm (6in) square of white Aida (Zweigart E3706), 14 blocks to 2.5cm (1in)

For the small picture: 15cm (6in) square of cream Damask Aida (Zweigart E3229), 14 blocks to 2.5cm (1in)

DMC STRANDED COTTON (FLOSS)

1 skein:	white	mid-grey 415
	raspberry 3733	raspberry 3731
	medium green 320	light green 368
	mint green 369	grey 414

1 Follow steps 1 and 2 for the Large Peacock.

2 The cross stitch in this design is worked using two strands of stranded cotton (floss), and the backstitch using one strand. Refer to the Stitch Guide on pages 10-11 for instructions on working the stitches. Work backstitch detail using grey 414 around each dove, making a small stitch for the beak and eye.

PEACOCKS AND TURTLE DOVES

THE *beautiful peacock is a member of the pheasant family and lives in the forest plains and foothills of India and Sri Lanka. Superstition towards them led to persecution and hunting in the past, leaving the bird very shy in the wild. In captivity, however, they are quite tame and have become a familiar sight throughout parks and gardens of the world. Only the male has the magnificent colouring and plumage, which is shed after breeding. The female is a dull brown in colour and half the size of the male.*

Turtle doves are pretty birds which used to be a common sight throughout Britain and were bred in special buildings called dovecotes which were owned by nobility and priests. The only time that most of us hear about them now, however, is in Christmas carols.

PEACOCK EVENING BAG

This stunning evening bag uses an abstract design which echoes the colours and shapes of peacock feathers. The iridescent hues have been picked out with metallic gold thread, highlighted by gold braid around the edge of the bag. The variety of threads and stitches makes this an interesting design to work. Some of the metallic threads are much thicker than embroidery silks, and so these have been worked using half cross stitch, which gives very quick results.

Finished design size: 13 x 21cm (5 x 8¼in) approximately using Aida, 14 blocks to 2.5cm (1in)

28 x 38cm (11 x 15in), black Aida (Zweigart E3706), 14 blocks to 2.5cm (1in)
34cm (³⁄₈yd) x 90cm (36in) wide emerald satin fabric
20 x 30cm (7¾ x 12in) iron-on heavyweight interfacing

34cm (³⁄₈yd) x 90cm (36in) wide lightweight polyester wadding (batting)
90cm (1yd) gold corded braid
Matching sewing thread
Clasp or snap fasteners

DMC STRANDED COTTON (FLOSS)
1 skein: black 310   lime green 907
             navy blue 823   deep emerald green
             deep green 909   699
             dark mint green 911

TWILLEYS GOLDUST 20
1 ball: shade 34

TWILLEYS GOLDFINGERING
1 ball: blue WG36   black WG 82
         gold WG 2

1 reel (spool) Madeira metallic thread emerald

1 Follow steps 1 and 2 for the Large Peacock.
2 When working with DMC stranded cotton (floss), use three strands of stranded cotton

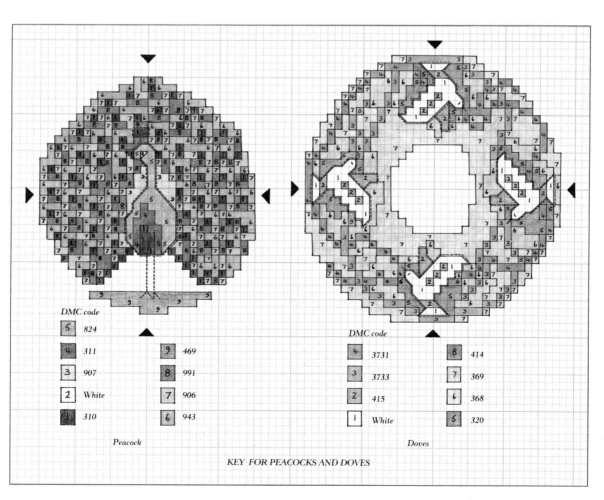

DMC code

5	824

4	311	9	469
3	907	8	991
2	White	7	906
	310	6	943

Peacock

DMC code

4	3731	8	414
3	3733	7	369
2	415	6	368
1	White	5	320

Doves

KEY FOR PEACOCKS AND DOVES

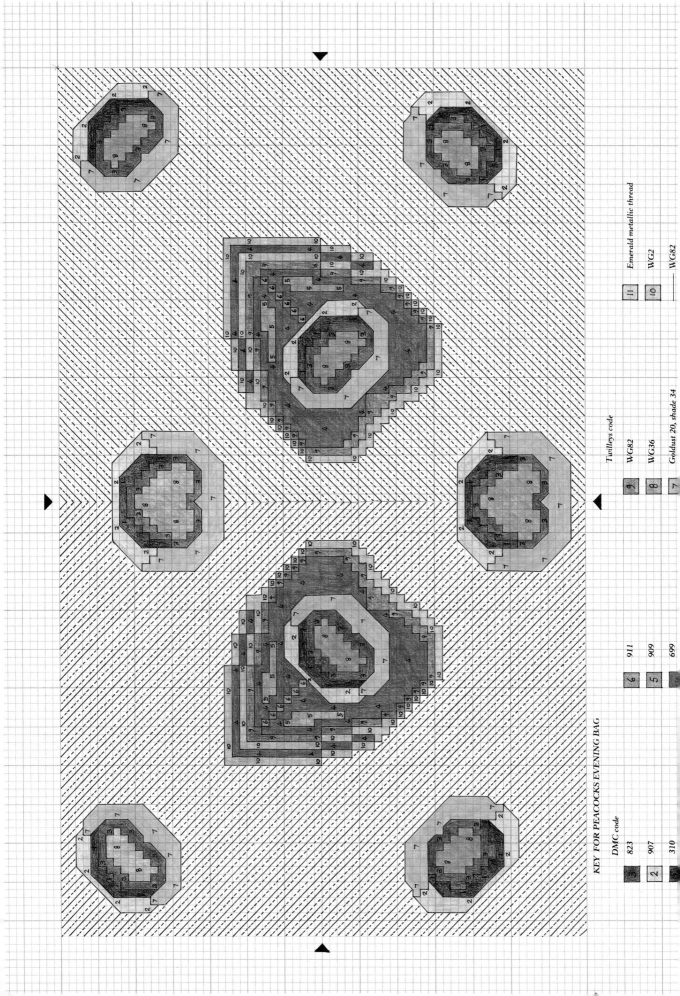

KEY FOR PEACOCKS EVENING BAG

DMC code

823
907
310

911
909
699

Twilleys code

WG82
WG36
Goldust 20, shade 34

Emerald metallic thread

WG2
WG82

(floss). For Twilleys Goldust use one strand of thread and for Twilleys Goldfingering work half cross stitch using one strand of thread. One full square on the chart indicates one half cross stitch. Refer to the Stitch Guide on pages 10-11 for instructions on working the stitches.

3 Backstitch is worked with Madeira metallic thread using two strands. For the background, the solid lines represent half cross stitch using Twilleys Goldfingering black WG 82 and the dotted lines represent backstitch using Madeira metallic thread. The direction of the lines indicates the direction of the stitches.

TO MAKE UP THE EVENING BAG

1 Work the design following the chart, and then press carefully on the wrong side. Trim the fabric around the design to within 1.5cm (⅝in).

2 Carefully iron the interfacing on to the back of the design to give added strength to the fabric and help keep the stitches secure.

3 Cut two pieces of satin fabric, one measuring 24 x 29cm (9½ x 11½in) and the other 24 x 41cm (9½ x 16¼in). Cut a piece of polyester wadding (batting) measuring 24 x 28cm (9½ x 11in). Place the smaller piece of satin on a flat surface, wrong side up. Lay the wadding (batting) on top, matching both long edges and one short edge with the satin. Pin and tack (baste) the wadding (batting) into place to form a padded satin piece. Fold the remaining satin at the short edge over the wadding (batting) and hem into place.

4 With right sides facing, match the upper long edge of the embroidered fabric with the unfinished short edge of the padded satin. Pin, tack (baste) and machine stitch along the seam line. Trim the wadding (batting) close to the seam line and then press the seam open.

5 With right sides facing, fold the padded satin in half so that the hemmed edge meets the seam line. Pin, tack (baste) and stitch along the outer edges, then trim away excess wadding (batting)

(Fig 1). Turn the pouch through to the right side. Press the remaining turnings of the embroidered fabric to the wrong side and hem into place. Hand stitch gold braid around the outer edge of the embroidered fabric, with the raw ends overlapping and facing inwards. (Refer to Fig 2 on page 23).

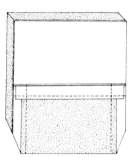

Fig 1 Stitching the bag

6 For the lining, take the remaining satin fabric and divide it into three along its length. Press a 1.5cm (⅝in) turning along both short edges. Fold over one-third of the length so that right sides are facing, then pin, tack (baste) and stitch along the outer edges (Fig 2). Press the turnings along the remaining edges and slip the lining inside the finished pouch. Match the edges of the lining and pouch together, pin and stitch in place. To finish the bag, stitch snap fasteners or a clasp at the corners of the flap to keep it securely in place.

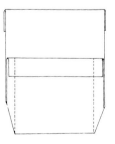

Fig 2 Stitching the lining

Swallows Bell Pull, Cushion and Picture

Swallows *traditionally herald the beginning of spring and these beautiful designs will remind you of springtime all year round. The complete design is used for the bell pull, and a single adult bird has been worked to fit the small brass picture frame. For the cushion, both adult birds are worked against the sky-blue background. For a humorous table runner or long picture, repeat the swallow chicks so that you have lots of them all sitting in a row.*

SWALLOWS BELL PULL

Finished design 13 x 51cm (5 x 20in) approximately using Aida, 14 blocks to 2.5cm (1in)

28 x 66cm (11 x 26in) white Aida (Zweigart E3706),
   14 blocks to 2.5cm (1in)
18 x 56cm (7 x 22in) matching cotton backing fabric
18cm (7in) bell-pull hanging rod
1.3m (1⅜yd) contrast furnishing braid
Matching sewing thread (contd page 110)

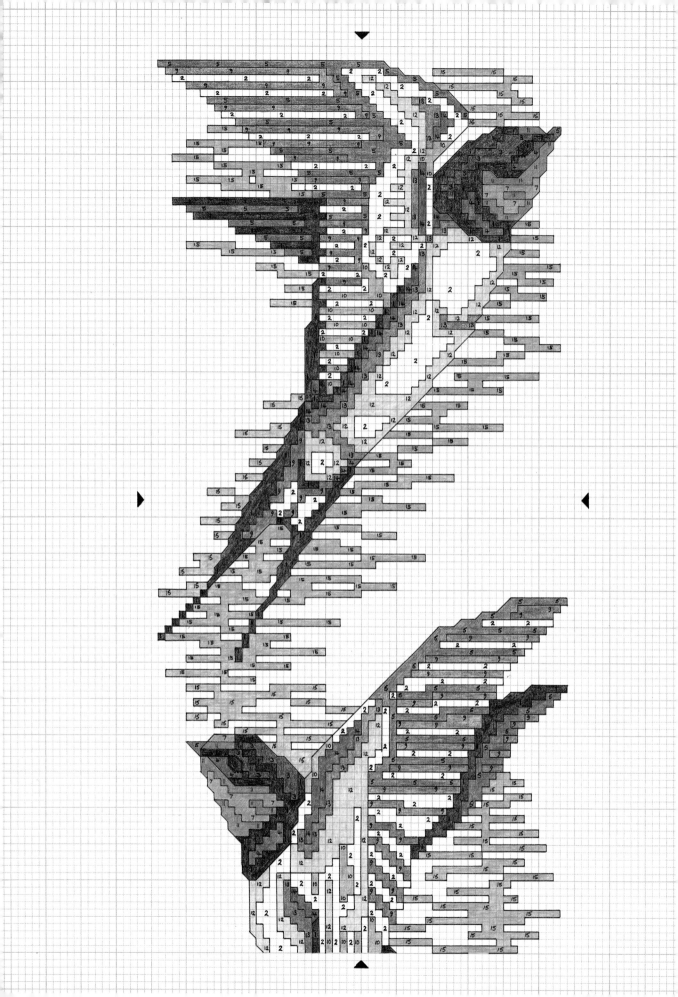

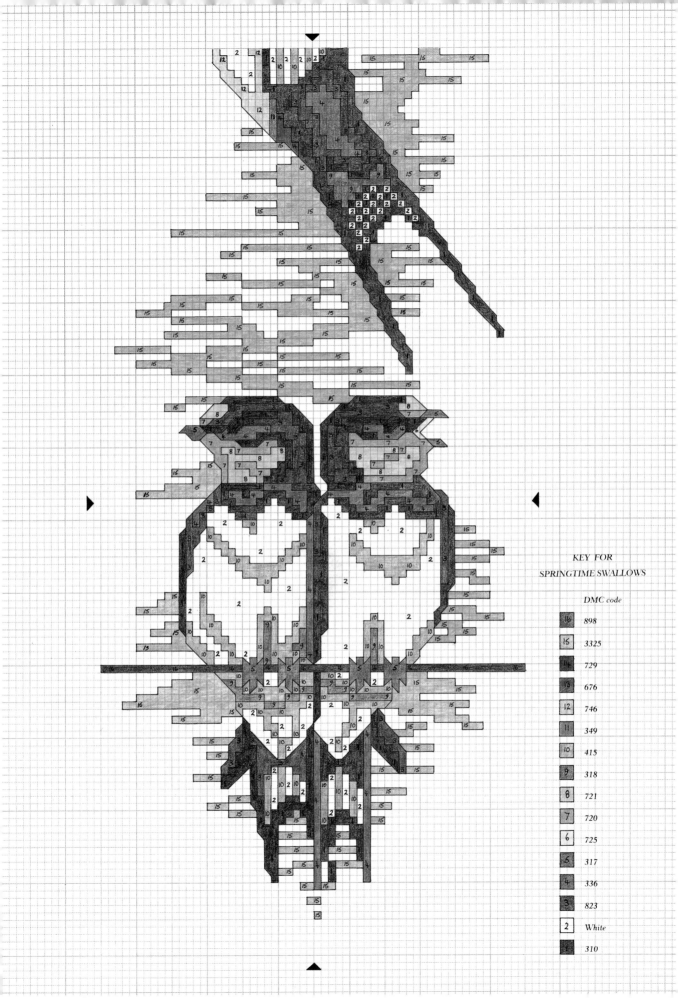

KEY FOR
SPRINGTIME SWALLOWS

DMC code

16	898
15	3325
14	729
13	676
12	746
11	349
10	415
9	318
8	721
7	720
6	725
5	317
4	336
3	823
2	White
1	310

DMC STRANDED COTTON (FLOSS)

1 skein:		
	black 310	white
	navy blue 823	navy blue 336
	grey 317	light gold 725
	rust 720	orange 721
	grey 318	light grey 415
	red 349	cream 746
	beige 676	beige 729
	light blue 3325	dark brown 898

1 Before you start stitching, read through Techniques on pages 8-9 for how to prepare your fabric, mark the centre point and start off your thread.

2 Match the tacking (basting) lines on the fabric with the arrows at the sides of the chart, and then work the design from the centre outwards.

3 The cross stitch in this design is worked using two strands of stranded cotton (floss), and the backstitch using one strand. Work backstitch detail using white around the eyes.

TO MAKE UP THE BELL PULL

1 The length of the bell-pull hanging rods determines the width of the fabric. The hanging rod used here allows for a 13cm (5in) wide strip. Purchase the rods before you start working the design to ensure that they will be wide enough. Follow the chart to work the design, allowing plenty of excess fabric around the edges. Press.

2 Mark the correct width and length of the bell pull on to the fabric with tacking (basting) lines. Cut the fabric, adding 1.5cm (^{5}⁄$_8$in) along both long and diagonal edges, and 5cm (2in) at the top edge. Press the turnings in place and mitre all corners (see Fig 2 for the Mallard Napkins on pages 30-2). Cut the backing fabric to the same size, but add a 1.5cm (^{5}⁄$_8$in) turning all the way round.

3 Hand stitch furnishing braid around both long and diagonal edges of the embroidered fabric. Position the hanging rod at the top of the strip, on the wrong side under the fold of the turning. Hand stitch the turning in place along the outer edges. Stitch the backing fabric in place.

SWALLOWS CUSHION

Finished design size: 33cm (13in) square approximately using Aida, 11 blocks to 2.5cm (1in)

36cm (14¼in) square sky Aida (Zweigart E1007), 11 blocks to 2.5cm (1in)

90cm (1yd) x 115cm (45in) wide, contrast cotton fabric for frill and backing
25.5cm (10in) zip
Matching sewing thread

DMC STRANDED COTTON (FLOSS)

1 skein:		
	black 310	navy blue 823
	navy blue 336	grey 317
	light gold 725	rust 720
	orange 721	grey 318
	light grey 415	red 349
	cream 746	beige 676
	beige 729	dark brown 898
2 skeins:	white	

1 Follow steps 1 and 2 for the Swallow Bell Pull.

2 The cross stitch in this design is worked using three strands of stranded cotton (floss) and the backstitch using one strand. Refer to the Stitch Guide on pages 10-11 for instructions on working the stitches. Work backstitch detail using white around the eyes.

3 Follow the designs for each adult bird and stitch one design in opposite corners. Work the sky by following the chart, then match up both sky areas by adding a few scattered cross stitches.

4 To make up the frilled cushion, follow the instructions for the Siamese Cat Cushion given on page 14. Follow steps 1, 2, 4 and 5 of the making-up instructions, but cut the template as described in step 1 to measure 36cm (14¼in) square.

SWALLOW PICTURE

Finished design size: 8 x 11cm (3 x 4¼in) approximately using Oslo, 22 threads to 2.5cm (1in)

23cm (9in) square white Oslo (Zweigart E3947), 22 blocks to 2.5cm (1in)

1 Follow the list of stranded cotton (floss) requirements given for the Swallow Bell Pull.

2 Follow steps 1 and 2 for the Swallow Bell Pull.

3 The cross stitch and backstitch in this design are worked using one strand of stranded cotton (floss). Work backstitch detail using white around the eyes.

4 When the stitching is complete, press carefully from the wrong side. Cut a piece of interfacing to the same size as the fabric, and iron on to the back.

5 Refer to Mounting and Framing on page 9 for instructions on completing your picture.

Ocean Waves Collection

Wɪᴛʜ the need to save the whale and other marine wildlife, the whale tail design seemed an obvious choice to include in this book. The playful dolphins, leaping through the water, are worked on two different sizes of Aida fabric. Alternatively, you could adapt the design by replacing the silk threads with small coloured glass beads, as for the spectacles case shown here. Finally, the penguin and tiny chick have been used to decorate a small trinket box; the design can also be seen on pages 114-15.

WHALE TAIL PAPERWEIGHT AND CARD

Finished design size: 8cm (3in) diameter approximately using Aida, 14 blocks to 2.5cm (1in)

23cm (9in) square of white Aida (Zweigart E3706), 14 blocks to 2.5cm (1in)

DMC STRANDED COTTON (FLOSS)

1 skein:
black 310
deep navy blue 939
aqua 958
light blue 3755

white
royal blue 312
blue 322

1 Before you start stitching your design, read through Techniques on pages 8-9 to find out how to prepare your fabric, mark the centre point and start off your thread.
2 Match the tacking (basting) lines with the centre of the chart, then work the design from the centre outwards.
3 The cross stitch in this design is worked using two strands of stranded cotton (floss), and the backstitch using one strand. Refer to the Stitch Guide on pages 10-11 for instructions on working the stitches. Work backstitch detail using black 310 all around the tail.
4 Refer to Mounting and Framing on page 9 for instructions on completing your project.

DOLPHIN TRINKET BOX AND CARD

Finished small design size: 8cm (3in) diameter approximately using Aida, 14 blocks to 2.5cm (1in)

23cm (9in) square of white Aida (Zweigart E3706), 14 blocks to 2.5cm (1in)

Finished large design size: 9cm (3½in) diameter approximately using Aida, 11 blocks to 2.5cm (1in)

23cm (9in) square of white Aida (Zweigart E1007), 11 blocks to 2.5cm (1in)

DMC STRANDED COTTON (FLOSS)

1 skein:
black 310
grey 414
royal blue 312
light blue 3755

white
grey 318
blue 322

1 Follow steps 1 and 2 for the Whale Tail design.
2 The cross stitch in this design is worked using two strands of stranded cotton (floss), the backstitch and French knots using one strand. Work backstitch detail using black 310 all around each fish and fins. The eye is worked with a French knot using black 310.
3 Refer to Mounting and Framing on page 9 for instructions on completing your project.

PENGUIN TRINKET BOX

Finished design size: 3 x 3.75cm (1¼ x 1½in) approximately using Aida, 14 blocks to 2.5cm (1in)

23cm (9in) square of white Aida (Zweigart E3706), 14 blocks to 2.5cm (1in)

DMC STRANDED COTTON (FLOSS)

1 skein:
black 310
grey 3022
dark orange 900

white
grey 414
pale lemon 3078

1 Follow steps 1 and 2 for the Whale Tail design.
2 The cross stitch and French knots in this design are worked using two strands of stranded cotton (floss), and the backstitch using one strand. Work backstitch detail using grey 414 around the adult's chest, the chick's beak and to mark the ground line. The eye is worked with a French knot using white.
3 Refer to Mounting and Framing on page 9 for instructions on completing your trinket box.

DOLPHIN BEADED SPECTACLES CASE

23 x 33cm (9 x 13in) white Aida (Zweigart E3706) 14 blocks to 2.5cm (1in)
23 x 45cm (9 x 17¾in) contrast cotton or silk fabric for backing and lining
Matching sewing thread
Sewing threads to match the beads
Two snap fasteners

MILL HILL BEADS (see Stockists)

1 pack antique beads	snow white 03015	pewter 03008
	slate blue 03010	
1 pack *seed beads*	black 02014	ice 02010
	light blue 00146	sapphire
	iris 00252	00168
frosted beads	crystal 60161 (see step 2)	

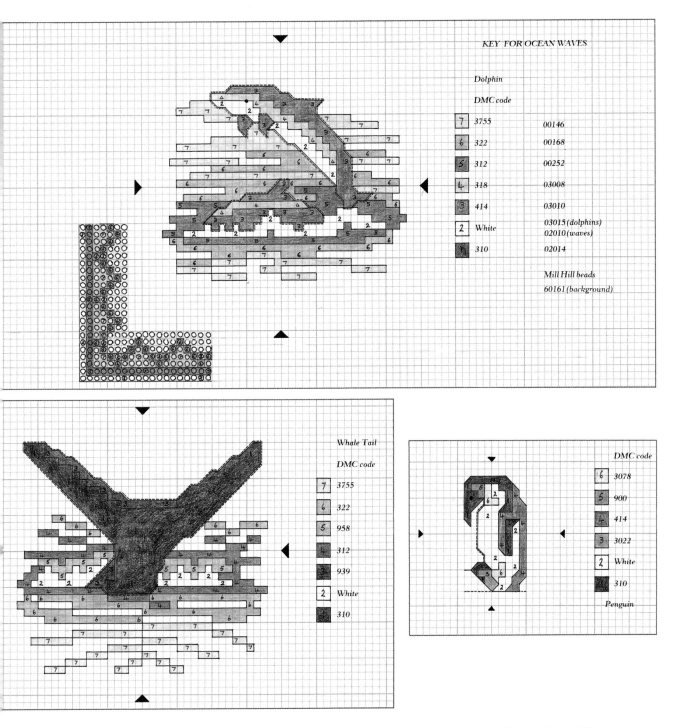

Dolphin

DMC code

7	3755	00146
6	322	00168
5	312	00252
4	318	03008
3	414	03010
2	White	03015 (dolphins) 02010 (waves)
	310	02014

Mill Hill beads
60161 (background)

Whale Tail

DMC code

7	3755
6	322
5	958
	312
	939
2	White
	310

DMC code

6	3078
5	900
4	414
3	3022
2	White
	310

Penguin

1 Follow steps 1 and 2 for the Whale Tail design.
2 The design as shown requires four packs of frosted beads in crystal 60161 for the background. The decorative border design is shown with the dolphin chart, and can be adapted to fit any size. 3 Refer to the Stitch Guide on pages 10-11 for instructions on working with beads. Use a matching coloured sewing thread to attach the beads. 4 Follow the dolphin chart, with each square now representing a bead instead of a cross stitch. Work half squares as one colour, using your judgement to decide which colour to use. Work the eye using a black bead instead of a French knot. The border and seagulls add the finishing touch.

TO MAKE UP THE SPECTACLES CASE
1 When the design is complete, trim away excess fabric to 1.5cm (⅝in). Cut a piece of backing fabric and two pieces of lining fabric to the same size.
2 To complete the case, follow the instructions for the Harvest Mice Spectacles Case given on page 23 following steps 2 and 4 of the making-up instructions.

Animal Magic Collection

THIS *collection of cute miniature animals was designed especially for children, either to stitch up themselves, or for adults to make charming gifts and accessories. Designs have been used to decorate simple gifts for children such as greetings cards, keyrings and a beautiful baby's cot blanket and matching cushion. The penguin design can also be seen on page 111, and the chart on page 113. Cross stitch, three-quarter cross stitch and backstitch are combined to add the intricate detail and character to each animal.*

BABY'S COT BLANKET

Finished design size: each animal is 5cm (2in) square approximately, using Afghan (Anne) evenweave fabric, 18 threads to 2.5cm (1in)

112 x 70cm (44 x 27½in) white Anne evenweave fabric (Zweigart E7563), 18 threads to 2.5cm (1in)
Matching sewing thread

1 Before you start stitching the design, read through Techniques on pages 8-9 to find out how to prepare your fabric, mark the centre point and start off your thread.
2 Match the tacking (basting) lines on the fabric with the arrows at the sides of the chart, and then work the design from the centre outwards.
3 Afghan (Anne) is a soft evenweave fabric which has tramlines running through it to create squares. The cross stitch in this design is worked using three strands of stranded cotton (floss) and the backstitch using one strand. Each cross stitch is worked over two threads. Refer to the Stitch Guide on pages 10-11 for instructions on working the stitches.

4 Cut a rectangle of fabric measuring 4 x 7 squares, adding an extra 5cm (2in) all the way round the outer edge to allow for fringing. Run several rows of machine stitches 5cm (2in) from the outer edge.
5 Stitch the designs by following the pattern layout (Fig 1). Alternatively, you could stitch the designs at random, or make up your own pattern.

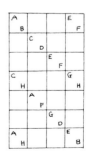

Fig 1 Pattern layout

To finish, make the fringing by teasing out the threads at the outer edges. The rows of machine stitches will prevent the fabric fraying further.

MINIATURE BELL PULL

Finished design size: each animal is 4.5cm (1¾in) square approximately using Aida, 14 blocks to 2.5cm (1in)

23 x 38cm (9 x 15in) white Aida (Zweigart E3706), 14 blocks to 2.5cm (1in)
23 x 38cm (9 x 15in) matching cotton fabric for backing
13cm (5in) bell-pull rods
Matching sewing thread

1 Follow steps 1 and 2 for the Baby's Cot Blanket.
2 The cross stitch in this design is worked using two strands of stranded cotton (floss) and the backstitch using one strand. Each cross stitch is worked over two threads. Refer to the Stitch Guide on pages 10-11 for instructions on working the stitches.
3 The finished size of the bell pull is 8 x 28cm (3 x 11in): the length of the bell-pull rods determines the width of the fabric. It is advisable to purchase the rods before working the design to ensure that they will be wide enough.
4 Mark the size of the finished bell pull on to the fabric with tacking (basting) lines, and then work the design, arranging animals at random. Trim excess fabric to 1.5cm (⅝in) at both long edges and 2.5cm (1in) at both short edges. Cut a piece of backing fabric to the same size, then press all turnings to the wrong side, secure the bell-pull rods at each end and stitch the backing fabric in place.

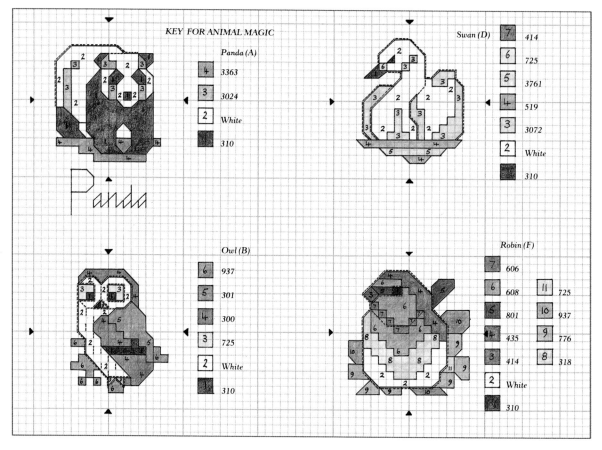

KEY FOR ANIMAL MAGIC

Panda (A)
4	3363
3	3024
2	White
	310

Swan (D)
7	414
6	725
5	3761
4	519
3	3072
2	White
	310

Owl (B)
6	937
5	301
4	300
3	725
2	White
	310

Robin (F)
7	606	11	725
6	608	10	937
5	801	9	776
4	435	8	318
3	414		
2	White		
	310		

DMC STRANDED COTTON (FLOSS)

Panda (A)
1 skein: black 310 white
grey 3024 green 3363

Work backstitch using black 310 around the back, top and side of head, under the tummy and for the writing.

Owl (B)
1 skein: black 310 white
light gold 725 dark copper 300
copper 301 moss green 937

Work backstitch using black 310 around the eyes, face, chest, feet and chest markings.

Cat (C)
1 skein: black 310 white
copper 301 tan 976
light tan 977 grey 3022
dark copper 300

Work backstitch using dark copper 300 around the body, back, head and tail.

Swan (D)
1 skein: black 310 white
light grey 3072 blue 519
light blue 3761 light gold 725
grey 414

Work backstitch using grey 414 around the body, neck and head.

Lion Cub (E)
1 skein: black 310 white
pink 776 brown 433
deep buff 435 buff 437
mid-green 3364 dark brown 898

Work backstitch using dark brown 898 around the body, paws, tail, head, eyes, nose and mouth.

Robin (F)
1 skein: black 310 white
grey 414 deep buff 435
dark brown 801 deep orange 608
red 606 grey 318
pink 776 moss green 937
light gold 725

Work backstitch using dark brown 801 around the body, tail, eye and head.

Squirrel (G)
1 skein: black 310 dark brown 898
copper 400 copper 3776
light copper 402 moss green 937

Work backstitch using dark brown 898 around the tail, body and feet.

Ladybird (H)
1 skein: black 310 white
red 606 dark orange 900
dark gold 782 moss green 937
lime green 907

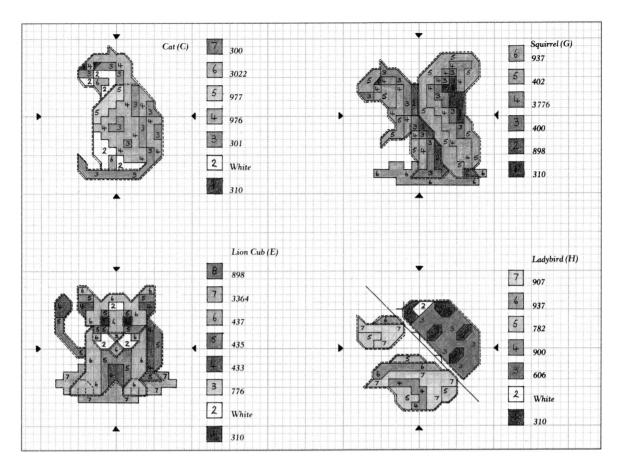

Cat (C)	
7	300
6	3022
5	977
4	976
3	301
2	White
	310

Squirrel (G)	
6	937
5	402
4	3776
3	400
2	898
1	310

Lion Cub (E)	
8	898
7	3364
6	437
5	435
4	433
3	776
2	White
	310

Ladybird (H)	
7	907
6	937
5	782
4	900
3	606
2	White
	310

Work backstitch using one strand of black 310 around the body and two strands for the legs and antennae. Use one strand of moss green 937 around the leaves and two strands of lime green 907 for the stalks.

BABY'S CUSHION

Finished design size: each animal is 5cm (2in) square approximately using Anne evenweave fabric, 18 threads to 2.5cm (1in)

34cm (13½in) square white Anne (Zweigart E7563) evenweave fabric, 18 threads to 2.5cm (1in)
34cm (13½in) square, cotton fabric for backing
3.5m (3⅞yd) white lace trim
Polyester wadding (batting) for filling
Matching sewing thread

1 Follow steps 1-3 for the Baby's Cot Blanket. Cut a square of Anne fabric measuring 2 x 2 squares, adding a 1.5cm (⅝in) seam allowance all the way round. Cut a piece of backing fabric to the same size.
2 Stitch one design at each outer and inner corner of the squares on the fabric. With right sides facing, pin, tack (baste) and stitch the cushion front and back together, leaving a 15cm (6in) gap for turning. Turn through to the right side, fill with wadding (batting), and secure the opening with slipstitch, then add a lace trim around the outer edges.

TRINKETS AND CARDS

Finished design size: each animal is 4.5cm (1¾in) square approximately using Aida, 14 blocks to 2.5cm (1in)

18cm (7in) square of white Aida (Zweigart E3706), 14 blocks to 2.5cm (1in)
Small scraps of lightweight iron-on interfacing

1 Follow steps 1 and 2 for the Baby's Cot Blanket.
2 The cross stitch in these designs is worked using two strands of stranded cotton (floss) and the backstitch using one strand. Refer to the Stitch Guide on pages 10-11 for instructions on working the stitches.
3 Refer to Mounting and Framing on page 9 for instructions on completing your trinkets or cards.

FROGS, SNAKES AND SNAILS

These comical little creatures are wonderful for adding colour and fun to children's gifts and accessories such as a bookmark, pencil case or headband. Most of the designs are worked up on Aida with 14 blocks to 2.5cm (1in), but you can experiment with different fabrics to make the designs larger or smaller, like the snail picture worked on Zweibinca (Zweigart E3712) or the tiny frog buttons worked on Lugana (Zweigart E3835), which is then stretched over plastic cover buttons.

FABRICS
Aida (Zweigart E3706), 14 blocks to 2.5cm (1in)
Zweibinca (Zweigart E3712), 6 blocks to 2.5cm (1in)
Lugana (Zweigart E3835), 25 threads to 2.5cm (1in)

DMC STRANDED COTTON (FLOSS)
Frogs
1 skein: black 310   white
         lime green 906   lime green 907
         light gold 725

Work backstitch using black 310 around the body, legs, eyes, pupils and top of the mouth.

Snails
1 skein: black 310   white
         dark tan 975   tan 976
         orange 742   grey 3022
         pale lemon 3078

Work backstitch using black 310 around the body, head and eyes, and round each band of colour on the shell.

Snakes
1 skein: black 310   white
         lime green 906   lime green 907
         lemon 307   red 606

Work backstitch using black 310 around the body, head, mouth, eyes and fangs. Use two strands of red 606 for the tongue and black 310 to work the eye using a French knot.

1 Follow steps 1 and 2 for the Baby's Cot Blanket.
2 The cross stitch in these designs is worked using two strands of stranded cotton (floss) and the backstitch using one strand. For the buttons, both cross stitch and backstitch are worked using one strand of stranded cotton (floss). Refer to the Stitch Guide on pages 10-11 for instructions on working the stitches.

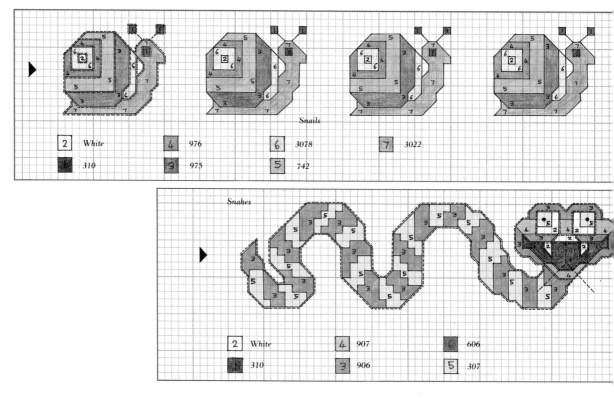

Snails

2	White	4	976	6	3078	7	3022
	310	3	975	5	742		

Snakes

2	White	4	907	6	606
	310	3	906	5	307

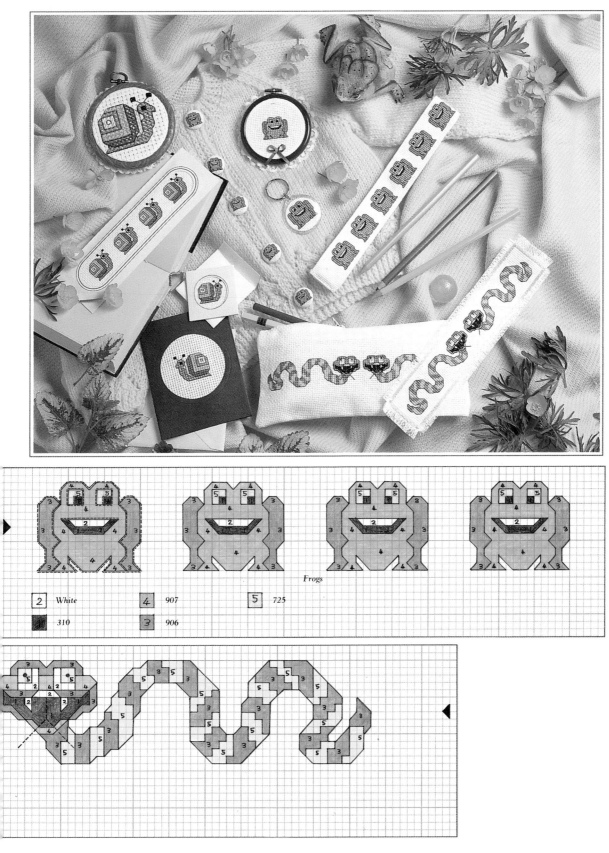

Frogs

2	White	4	907	5	725
■	310	3	906		

Butterflies and Bumble Bees Gifts

THIS *charming collection of butterflies and bumble bees will provide you with hours of inspired stitching. Altogether, there are eight brightly coloured designs of butterflies fluttering along the hedgerows and busy bees buzzing around summer fruits. As each design is small and simple, they are ideal to use on their own or mixed with any of the others. Try decorating gifts or simple accessories, such as pot-pourri sachets and pillows, hand towels, trinket boxes and cards.*

BUTTERFLY APRON

Finished design size: 8cm (3in) diameter approximately using Aida, 11 blocks to 2.5cm (1in)

43 x 66cm (17 x 26in) white Aida (Zweigart E1007), 11 blocks to 2.5cm (1in)
50cm (⅝yd) x 115cm (45in) wide contrast cotton floral fabric
Matching sewing thread

(contd)

DMC STRANDED COTTON (FLOSS)

Peacock

1 skein: black 310   white
          moss green 937   mid-green 3364
          dark purple 327   light gold 725
          dark orange 900   dark copper 300
          medium coffee 420   dark brown 801

Small Tortoiseshell

1 skein: black 310   white
          moss green 937   dark orange 900
          light gold 725   deep buff 435
          dark copper 300   dark brown 801
          turquoise 996   dark green 986
          lime green 905   deep yellow 743
          pink 776   light rose 3713

Painted Lady

1 skein: black 310   white
          moss green 937   deep buff 435
          turquoise 996   dark copper 300
          orange 971   red 606
          raspberry 3350   light rose 3713
          green 3363   mid-green 3364
          dark green 986   lime green 905

Red Admiral

1 skein: black 310   white
          moss green 937   dark green 986
          lime green 905   deep yellow 743
          turquoise 996   dark brown 801
          dark copper 300   red 606
          buff 437

1 Before you start stitching the design, read through Techniques on pages 8-9 to find out how to prepare your fabric, mark the centre point and start off your thread.

2 Match the tacking (basting) lines on the fabric with the arrows at the sides of the chart, and then work the design from the centre outwards.

3 The cross stitch in this design is worked using three strands of stranded cotton (floss) and the backstitch using one strand. Refer to the Stitch Guide on pages 10-11 for instructions on working the stitches.

4 Work backstitch detail around each butterfly and antenna using black 310. For the peacock use mid-green 3364 to work the flower stems; for the small tortoiseshell, work backstitch detail using deep buff 435 for each petal and flower centre; and finally, for the red admiral, use buff 437 to work around each petal and flower centre.

5 Round off the corners of the Aida rectangle along one long edge, to form the lower edge of the apron. Along the lower edge, stitch a small tortoiseshell at each rounded corner, working the butterfly only, and a red admiral at the centre. Position each design roughly 6cm (2¼in) from the outer edges. For the pockets, work each of the remaining two designs on a piece of Aida measuring 15cm (6in) square.

TO MAKE UP THE APRON

1 For the frill, cut three strips from the floral fabric each measuring 115cm (45in) by 8.5cm (3¼in). For the waistband, cut a 10 x 61cm (4 x 24in) strip, and for the ties cut two pieces 12 x 56cm (4¾ x 22in). For the pocket binding, cut two strips each measuring 4.5 x 15cm (1¾ x 6in)

2 Bind the upper edges of the pockets with the floral fabric strips, then press a 1.5cm (⅝in) turning on the remaining three edges and stitch in place.

3 To make the frill, stitch the strips of fabric together to form one long strip, and hem one long edge by hand or machine. Machine stitch two lines of gathering threads along the length, then gather the frill to fit around both short edges and the lower edge of the apron. With right sides facing, pin, tack (baste) and machine stitch in place.

4 Finish by gathering the upper edge of the Aida to 28cm (11in), making sure not to gather the top frill edge, and then attach the waistband. Neaten the edges of the ties and stitch to the waistband.

BUTTERFLY HAND TOWEL

Finished design size: 5cm (2in) square approximately, using Aida, 15 blocks to 2.5cm (1in)

10cm (4in) white Aida band with white edging (Zweigart E7195), 15 blocks to 2.5cm (1in) to match width of towel
Hand towel
Narrow ribbon and lace for edging
Matching sewing thread

1 Follow the list of stranded cotton (floss) requirements given for the Butterfly Apron.

2 Follow steps 1 and 2 for the Butterfly Apron.

3 The cross stitch in this design is worked using

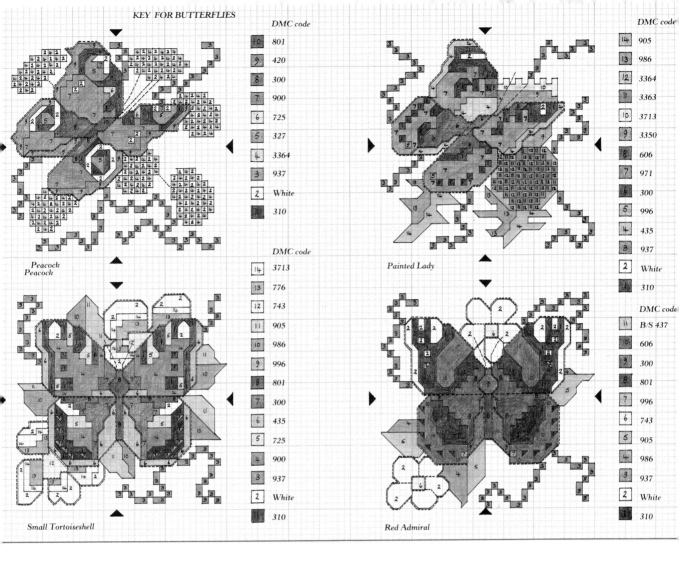

KEY FOR BUTTERFLIES

Peacock

	DMC code
10	801
9	420
8	300
7	900
6	725
5	327
4	3364
3	937
2	White
	310

Painted Lady

	DMC code
14	905
13	986
12	3364
11	3363
10	3713
9	3350
8	606
7	971
6	300
5	996
4	435
3	937
2	White
1	310

Small Tortoiseshell

	DMC code
14	3713
13	776
12	743
11	905
10	986
9	996
8	801
7	300
6	435
5	725
4	900
3	937
2	White
	310

Red Admiral

	DMC code
11	B/S 437
10	606
9	300
8	801
7	996
6	743
5	905
4	986
3	937
2	White
1	310

two strands of stranded cotton (floss) and the backstitch using one strand. Refer to the Stitch Guide on pages 10-11 for instructions on working the stitches. For backstitch detail, follow step 4 for the Butterfly Apron.

4 Cut the Aida band to the width of the hand towel, adding a 6mm (¼in) turning at each end. Work the designs, then press the band from the wrong side, pressing the turnings at each end. Machine stitch the band to the hand towel, then stitch lace trim along each long edge of the band. Finish by stitching narrow ribbon over the seam of the lace and add ribbon bows at each corner of the band.

SMALL LACY CUSHION

Finished design size: 5cm (2in) diameter approximately, using Aida, 11 blocks to 2.5cm (1in)

Cream Schönfels damask fabric (Zweigart E2144) or Aida with 11 blocks to 2.5cm (1in)

Cream lace for edging
Wadding (batting) for filling
Matching sewing thread

1 Follow the list of stranded cotton (floss) requirements given for the Butterfly Apron.
2 Follow steps 1 and 2 for the Butterfly Apron.
3 The cross stitch in this design is worked using three strands of stranded cotton (floss) and the backstitch using one strand. Refer to the Stitch Guide on pages 10-11 for instructions on working the stitches. For backstitch detail, follow Step 4 for the Butterfly Apron.
4 Work a single butterfly on to the fabric, then cut two circular shapes to the required size of your cushion. Place the pieces with right sides together and machine stitch 1.5cm (⅝in) from the outer edge, leaving a 10cm (4in) gap for turning. Turn the cushion through to the right side, stuff with wadding (batting) and then slipstitch the gap to close. Finish by stitching lace around the outer edge of the cushion.

DRAWSTRING BAG

Finished design size: 5cm (2in) diameter approximately using Aida, 11 blocks to 2.5cm (1in)

Cream Schönfels damask fabric (Zweigart E2144), or Aida, 11 blocks to 2.5cm (1in)
Cream bias tape
Cream twisted cord trim
Cream lace for edging
Matching sewing thread

1 Follow the list of stranded cotton (floss) requirements given for the Butterfly Apron.
2 Follow steps 1 and 2 for the Butterfly Apron.
3 The cross stitch in this design is worked using three strands of stranded cotton (floss) and the backstitch using one strand. For backstitch detail, follow step 4 for the Butterfly Apron.
4 Work a single butterfly on to the fabric, and then cut two rectangles of fabric to the required size. Place the rectangles with right sides together and machine stitch along the side edges to form a tube. When stitching the seam, leave a 1cm (½in) gap approximately 7cm (2¾in) from the top edge to form a small opening.
5 To make the casing for the drawstrings, stitch a length of bias tape across each width on the wrong side of the fabric, level with the gaps in the side seams. Machine stitch the circular fabric to the bottom edge of the tube to form the base. Thread two lengths of cord through the casing for the drawstrings. Hem the top edges, and then add the lace trim to finish.

BUTTERFLY TRINKETS

The trinket box, pincushion and greetings cards are all worked on white Aida (Zweigart E3706), 14 blocks to 2.5cm (1in). Refer to Mounting and Framing on page 9 for instructions on completing your trinket box, pincushion or cards.

BUMBLE BEE
POT-POURRI PILLOW

Finished design size: 5cm (2in) square approximately using damask Aida, 14 blocks to 2.5cm (1in)

Cream damask Aida (Zweigart E3229), 14 blocks to 2.5cm (1in)
Matching cotton fabric for backing
Cream lace for edging
Decorative lace for central panel
Cream or white fine net
Cream or white ribbon
Wadding (batting) for filling
Matching sewing thread
Paper for template
Pot-pourri or dried herbs

DMC STRANDED COTTON (FLOSS)

1 skein:		
	black 310	white
	olive green 581	raspberry 3350
	pink 899	deep purple 550
	dark lilac 208	red 606
	bright red 666	orange 741
	orange 742	pale yellow 745
	lemon 307	lemon 445
	deep yellow 743	

1 Follow steps 1 and 2 for the Butterfly Apron.
2 The cross stitch in this design is worked using two strands of stranded cotton (floss) and the backstitch using one strand. Work backstitch detail using black 310 around the bee's body, wings and legs.
3 Make a template for the pillow by drawing a square to the required size on a piece of paper. For each template shape, remember to add a 1.5cm (⅝in) seam allowance all the way round. Cut out one shape from backing fabric.
4 Using the template, mark the centre of each edge and then join the points with a diagonal line across each corner, creating a square and four triangles. Cut out the shapes to use as templates and then cut four triangles from damask Aida. Stitch bumble bees at random on each triangle.
5 From the remaining square template, cut one square from lace and two squares from fine net. Stitch the net squares together, leaving a small opening. Fill the pouch with pot-pourri and close the gap. Stitch the long edges of the damask triangles to each edge of the lace square, hiding the seams with ribbon. With right sides facing, stitch the cushion front and back together, leaving a gap for turning. Turn to right side.
6 Position the pot-pourri pouch inside the cushion and secure each corner to those of the lace insert. Fill the cushion with wadding (batting) and slipstitch the gap to close. Finish by stitching lace around the outer edges.

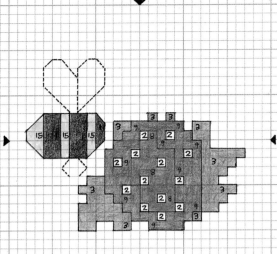

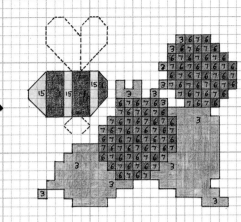

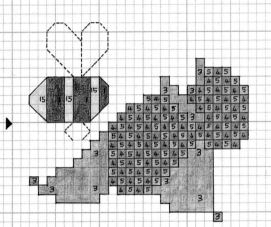

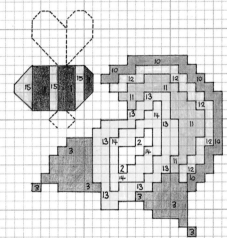

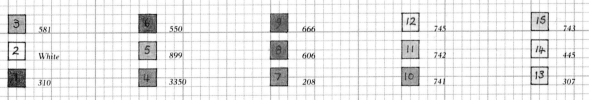

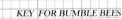

KEY FOR BUMBLE BEES

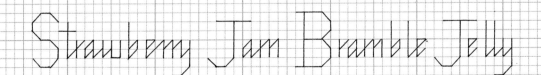

3 — 581	6 — 550	9 — 666	12 — 745	15 — 743
2 — White	5 — 899	8 — 606	11 — 742	14 — 445
1 — 310	4 — 3350	7 — 208	10 — 741	13 — 307

Strawberry Jam Bramble Jelly

Marmalade Raspberry

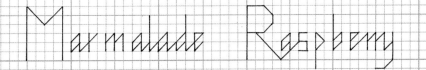

BUMBLE BEE POT-POURRI SACHETS

Finished design size: 5cm (2in) square approximately using damask Aida, 14 blocks to 2.5cm (1in)

Cream damask Aida (Zweigart E3229), 14 blocks to 2.5cm (1in)
Matching cotton fabric for backing
Cream lace for edging
Coloured ribbon
Matching sewing thread

1 Follow the list of stranded cotton (floss) given for the Bumble Bee Pot-pourri Pillow.
2 Follow steps 1 and 2 for the Butterfly Apron.
3 The cross stitch in this design is worked using two strands of stranded cotton (floss) and the backstitch using one strand. Refer to the Stitch Guide on pages 10-11 for instructions on working the stitches. Work backstitch detail using black 310 around bee's body, wings and legs.
4 Work the designs on to the fabric and then cut to the required size, adding a 6mm (¼in) seam allowance all the way round. Cut backing pieces to the same size. With right sides facing, stitch the front and back pieces together along three sides, leaving the top edge open. Turn through to the right side and edge with lace. Fill each sachet with dried herbs or pot-pourri, and tie with a pretty ribbon bow. The sachets can be used to scent wardrobes and drawers or as decorations.

BUMBLE BEE TEA TOWEL

Green Nina (Zweigart E7534), 8 blocks to 2.5cm (1in)

1 Follow the list of stranded cotton (floss) requirements given for the Bumble Bee Pot-pourri Pillow. Cut the fabric to the required size, then turn a 1cm (½in) hem all around, and machine stitch in place.
2 Nina is a thick fabric with an Aida strip running through it. Follow steps 1 and 2 for the Butterfly Apron.
3 The cross stitch in this design is worked using three strands of stranded cotton (floss) and the backstitch using two strands. Refer to the Stitch Guide on pages 10-11 for instructions on working the stitches. Work backstitch detail using black 310 around the bee's body, wings and legs.

BUMBLE BEE JAM-POT COVERS

These pretty jam-pot covers have been worked on Aida (Zweigart E3706), 14 blocks to 2.5cm (1in). Stitch the design following steps 1 and 2 for the Bumble Bee Pot-pourri Pillow, cut a circle to the required size, and then edge with lace.

Stockists

If you should require any further information about products, catalogues, price lists or local stockists from any of the suppliers mentioned below, please contact them direct by post or phone. Remember always to include a stamped addressed envelope. If you contact them by phone, they will be able to tell you if there is any charge for the catalogue or price lists.

DMC Creative World, Pullman Road, Wigston, Leicester LE18 2DY, Tel: 0533 811040.
Telephone for the name and address of your nearest DMC stockists.
Zweigart and DMC products are also supplied in the USA by:
The DMC Corporation, Port Kearny, Building 10, South Kearny, NJ 07032, USA.

Framecraft Miniatures Ltd, 372-376 Summer Lane, Hockley, Birmingham B19 3QA. Tel: (021) 212 0551.
Framecraft products are also supplied worldwide by:
Anne Brinkley Designs Inc, 761 Palmer Avenue, Holmdel, NJ 97733, USA.
Gay Bowles Sales Inc, PO Box 1060, Janesville, WI 53547, USA.
Ireland Needlecraft Pty Ltd, 4, 2-4 Keppel Drive, Hallam, Vic 3803, Australia.

Laura Ashley Customer Services, 150 Bath Road, Maidenhead, Berkshire, SL6 4YS. Tel: 0628 770345.
Laura Ashley have stores based worldwide, but if you have any enquiries, contact:

Laura Ashley Customer Services, 6 St James Avenue, 10th Floor, Boston, MA 02116, USA. Tel: 617 457 6000
Laura Ashley Customer Services, 24 Luchthavenweg, PO Box 7100, 5500LC Veldhoven, Netherlands. Tel: (40) 563111.

MacGregor Designs, PO Box 129, Burton upon Trent, DE14 3XH. Tel: (0283) 702117.
Telephone for mail order catalogue.

Twilleys of Stamford, Customer Service, Roman Mill, Stamford, Lincolnshire PE9 1BG.
Write for your nearest stockist.

Vilene interfacing products are available in major department stores and all good haberdashery shops.

Newey plastic cover buttons and **Panda Ribbons** are available from all major department stores and good needlework shops. If you have any queries, telephone 0449 740211 for further details.

Office Interiors, 407 Green Lanes, Palmers Green, London N13 4JD. Tel: 081 886 6481.

Some of the designs included in this book are available in kit form by mail. For further details contact:
The Janlynn Corporation, 34 Front Street, PO Box 51848, Indian Orchard, MA 01151-5848, USA.

At the time of publication, the following kits were available: Zebra Head, Walking Tiger, Cheetah and Cubs, Thomas Cat, Pheasant, Siamese Kittens and Siamese Cat (available as part of the 'Coming and Going' series).

ACKNOWLEDGEMENTS

We would like to say a special thank you to our husbands Ian and Tim, and to our families, for being so patient and putting up with us as the deadline approached.

We would also like to thank the following people for their contributions and help with getting this book published on time. Vivienne Wells, Brenda Morrison and Kay Ball at David & Charles for their expert help and advice with the production of the book – a special thank you to Vivienne, who introduced us to each other.

Thank you also to the following people and suppliers for their help and generosity:

Doreen Newey for contributing her superb knitting skills. Cara Ackerman, Jane Chamberlain, Maria Diaz and Tracey Loach of DMC Creative World for all their expert help and advice and for supplying all embroidery fabrics, stranded cotton (floss) and tapestry wool (yarn); greetings cards; circular, fluted and square paperweights (pages 31, 100-1, 115, 119, 120); trinket box (pages 100-1), plastic flexi-hoops (page 119), embroidery hoop; thread organiser and project cards (page 7).

Sarah Gray of Framecraft Miniatures Ltd, for supplying the wooden tea tray (page 26-7); glass coasters (pages 80-1); pendant; handbag mirror; gold flexi-frame (pages 100-1), oval brass frame, bell-pull rods (page 106-7), trinket box paperweight and Mill Hill beads (page 111), bookmark, gift tags, keyrings, fridge magnet, trinket box, square paperweight (pages 115, 119), and the hand-cut crystal bowl (page 120).

Laura Ashley for the fabrics used to complement some of the designs, (pages 2, 12-13, 26-7, 44-5, 70-1, 80-1, 106, 120).

Wendy Crease of Top Stitch Publicity for her help and support, and for supplying Newey plastic cover buttons and Panda Ribbons, used throughout the book.

MacGregor Designs for supplying the beautiful hand crafted footstool pages 44-5 and pincushion, page 120.

Jen Wade at Twilleys of Stamford for the metallic threads used for the Peacock Evening Bag, page 100-1.

Susan Haigh of Freudenberg for the Vilene interfacings used throughout the book.

Umit and Nanish Patel of Office Interiors for supplying office stationery and computer accessories.

Index